A
TRUER
GOD

Copyright © 2010 By Robert Bowie Johnson Jr. and the Concordant Publishing Concern. ISBN 978-0-9705438-6-8

Solving Light Books
727 Mount Alban Drive
Annapolis, MD 21409

SolvingLight.com, ATruerGod.com

Concordant Publishing Concern
15570 Knochhaven Road
Santa Clarita, CA 91387

Concordant.org

A
TRUER
GOD

The Supreme Spirit of Light and Love
in the
Hebrew and Greek Scriptures

Robert Bowie Johnson, Jr.

with writings of A. E. Knoch and other contributors
to *Unsearchable Riches* magazine
incorporated into the text.

Acknowledgments

Thanks to Frank Bonarrigo, Michael Thompson, Mark Wadsworth, Nancy Beth Fisher, Lisa Marone, Matt Franko, and Charles Rutsch. Please also see "Afterthoughts and Credits" on page 141.

For Nancy Lee

A TRUER GOD

The Supreme Spirit of Light and Love
in the
Hebrew and Greek Scriptures

CONTENTS

I.	The False God of Christian Myth	7
II.	The True God of the Sacred Scriptures	11
III.	Mistranslation—A Cloak of Deception	15
IV.	Hell—A Doctrine of Demons	23
V.	The Riddle, the Taboo, and the Threat	31
VI.	The True God's Time—the Eons	39
VII.	The Purpose of the Eons	47
VIII.	God's Creative Original	51
IX.	The First Eon—the Celestials	57
X.	The Disruption of the First World-System	61
XI.	The Second Eon—Mankind	67
XII.	The Deluge	81
XIII.	The Third Eon—Man's Day	85
XIV.	The Snatching Away of the Ecclesia	91
XV.	The Day of Indignation	101
XVI.	The Millennial Eon	107
XVII.	The Great White Throne Judgment	117
XVIII.	The Eon of the Eons	127
XIX.	The Consummation—the End of the Eons	135
XX.	A Scriptural Summary	139
XXI.	Afterthoughts and Credits	141

Dedication

To the memory of A. E. Knoch and Vladimir Michael Gelesnoff, founders of the Concordant Publishing Concern. Their faithfulness made this book possible.

Chapter I

THE FALSE GOD OF CHRISTIAN MYTH

In the beginning, the God of Christian myth created Adam and Eve in the Garden of Eden desiring for them eternal happiness. But God had also created a perfect angel by the name of Lucifer. He was the "Anointed Cherub" who led the celestial hosts in praise and worship. But one day, Lucifer became full of pride and fell into sin, desiring worship for himself. He became the Devil, contaminating other perfect angels who themselves became demons. Lucifer's rebellion surprised and disappointed God.

Lucifer hated Adam and Eve and so decided to trick them into disobeying God whom he also hated. In the guise of the serpent, he was able to convince the first two humans to eat the forbidden fruit of the Tree of the Knowledge of Good and Evil. God became surprised and disappointed with Adam and Eve also. Since by their own choice, they had welcomed sin and evil into the human race, He was forced to curse them and their descendants with lives of toil ending in death. Thus Lucifer, abetted by the perverse will of our first parents, ruined God's wonderful plans for mankind.

Lucifer, under the name of Satan, became the overseer of a place created by God for the eternal torment of human souls after death called Hell. But God wished that Adam and Eve and all of their descendants could be saved from such a horrible fate. God was lucky enough to have a Son who, being purposed to die on Calvary, could at least salvage a certain percentage of humanity from the Hell fires of everlasting torture. Since the time of Adam, the best that God can do is appeal and beg and plead with sinners so that He at least gets some in heaven, otherwise the Devil gets them all in Hell.

But at the same time also, the Devil—the most deceptive and subtle of all God's creatures—appeals to sinners not to accept Christ, and thus entraps as many as he can in endless despair. God, mainly through church pulpits and radio and television preachers, continues to battle with Satan, trying to get as many humans as possible saved and into heaven.

God foresaw the existence of all the billions of human beings when He created Adam and Eve. He realized what a big gamble it was—for most of these beings would wind up in everlasting anguish because of the Devil. Yet He went ahead with Adam's and Eve's creation anyway because at least some of their descendants would be able to enjoy eternal bliss with Him in heaven.

Then for some reason, at the tower of Babel, He deliberately confounded the one language of the world into many, and made it that much harder for heathens and sinners to find out what they need to do to be saved. How much easier it would have been to save the lost if we all had continued to speak just one language!

Then, during the Dark Ages, either God would not or could not give to the world which He "so loved" printed Bibles, tracts, radios, printing presses, etc., to keep them from the Devil's bondage. And even to this day, with all these things, millions of heathens are not reached who, for the most part, must be lost, or Christendom would not be sending missionaries and money to the foreign fields.

Throughout human history, the God of Christendom works a few miracles here and there but, generally speaking, average people don't get to see one, even though such an event would greatly help their ability to believe in Him. And stranger yet, God saves His greatest miracle for last, after earth's history ends and He has lost the battle for the most souls to Satan. He keeps billions of souls alive and conscious forever in a tormenting fire that never goes out and yet never consumes its victims. This greatest of supernatural marvels is also the most spectacular display of hatred and vengeance ever in the universe. Infinite suffering becomes the punishment for finite transgressions. Ultimately, the God of Christendom spends more of his energy seeing to the torment of human souls than doing anything else. What glory the miserable sound of billions of wailing lungs and gnashing teeth brings to Him we are not told.

Despite all the pulpit talk of peace, love, grace, truth, and light, the basic and unmistakable message to humanity from the God of Christendom seems indistinguishable from extortion— "Obey Me or burn!"

It is indeed sad, but the majority of mankind, abetted by Satan, turn out to be more determined to be lost than God is determined to save them. Instead of winding up mankind's destiny to the good, the so-called "God of Love" keeps on tormenting most of His creations for eternity. A shattered universe, not a reconciled and harmonious one, crowns the efforts of the Almighty God and the intervention in human history of His Anointed One, Jesus Christ.

Questions about the plans and purpose of the God of Christendom, and about Christendom itself do arise.

How can anyone be "happy" in God's heaven knowing that one or more family members—wife, husband, brother, sister, mother, father, son, daughter—is trapped in punishment and suffering without end?

Why is it wrong for us to torment our own children for even a short time but okay for God to torment many of His forever?

If God is Love and Love never fails, why is it that God's Love does not apply to those who need it most?

Why can't the Creator master His Own creatures?

Why isn't God powerful enough to overcome the powers of evil that have estranged His creatures from Him?

Why is He not wise enough to lure the rebellious back to Himself?

Wouldn't a random universe with no purpose at all be far more benign than the universe created by the God of orthodoxy? If we evolved from some kind of primordial slime, we'll probably devolve back into it, and just cease to exist. In the end, there will be no anguish, no torment, just nothingness. Isn't this much to be preferred over the end the God of Christendom has in view—a few happy souls and billions of suffering ones, cursing God, their Creator, forever?

Why do humans welcome the birth of children with great joy? If there's even a slim chance of a precious newborn eventually winding up in eternal torment, shouldn't we be weeping at that horrible prospect?

Why does much of Christendom oppose abortion when it is a sure way to counteract the awful possibility of a soul's unending agony?

And why do they oppose homosexual unions? Same-sex marriages may be unnatural but at least they do not bring foredoomed souls into the world.

When we begin to ask these kinds of questions, we are told to be quiet and just believe in this weak, failing, blundering, and fiendish God of popular Christendom.

After all this bad news, the good news is that this object of worship presented to us by the theologians and gospelizers is, indeed, a God of myth, and not of the Scriptures. The True God is much different, thank God.

Chapter II

THE TRUE GOD OF THE SACRED SCRIPTURES

Superexcessively above and beyond the best intentions of the amiable adventurer of Christendom, who wants to save everybody but is unable to do so, the True God has a purpose worthy of the One Who created the universe and all the life that is in it. He is Supreme. In the Hebrew Scriptures, He is *El* which means Subjector; in the Greek Scriptures, He is *Theos* which means Placer. He is the Supreme Subjector and Placer of all. He "wills that all mankind be saved and come into a realization of the truth" (I Timothy 2:4), and He is "operating all in accord with the counsel of His will" (Ephesians 1:11). The will of the Almighty is paramount. There is no man or spirit who can withstand it. He is "Declaring the end from the beginning, and from ancient times the things that are not yet done, saying, My counsel shall stand, and I will do all my pleasure" (Isaiah 46:10).

What do we know of God's essential being? He is Spirit (John 4:24), He is Light (I John 1:5), and He is Love (I John 4:8). Since all is out of God (Romans 11:36), then creation is out of Spirit, Light, and Love—Love which purposes, Light which reveals, and Spirit which energizes. Can we even imagine Spirit and Light intending a final darkness for much of humanity? Can we entertain for a second that Love will take pleasure in even a single creature's unending anguish? Let us consider these very direct and simple words from the apostle Paul:

Faithful is the saying and worthy of all welcome (for for this are we toiling and being reproached), that we rely on the living God, Who is the Saviour of all mankind, especially of believers. These things be charging and teaching (I Timothy 4:9-11).

Perhaps in all the annals of human history, no declaration so deserving of acceptance has been so neglected or opposed as this—that

God is the Saviour of all mankind. Yet, as we see from the context, the assertion that the living God, or True God, is the Saviour of all mankind, especially of believers, is *faithful*; that is, unfailing and dependable. The saying is *worthy of all welcome*. This means we should embrace it and believe it. True, all of God's words are faithful and call for eager acceptance within their context, but here is a saying marked off with special emphasis and magnified with special importance.

Paul further instructs Timothy to be *charging and teaching* this marvelous precept. This means it is a foundational truth of Christianity. The True God, the Supreme Subjector and Placer, is not just the Saviour of a few, or of some, or of many, or of most, but of *all mankind*. It is clear also from the context that believers enjoy an especial place—not an exclusive one—in the plans and purpose of the True God.

Those who are part of the body of Christ are saved prior to the rest. They will be made like their Lord at the time of His appearing for them in the air. They will live and reign with Christ during the coming eons, or ages. They will not be brought into judgment at the time of the great white throne described in chapter twenty of Revelation. Believers are not subject to the second death.

Those who do not believe now will be raised up at the time of the great white throne and will be judged and dealt with according to their deeds. Then all whose names are not written in the book of life will be cast into the lake of fire that is the second death—not a place of punishment, but of sleep, unconsciousness and oblivion.

After this, at the end of the eons, God will abolish death, all death, and impart the resurrection life of Christ to all. Then it will be clear that God is indeed the Saviour of all. Other Scriptures reveal what is included in this salvation. God will JUSTIFY ALL (Romans 5:18, 19). He will RECONCILE ALL to Himself (Colossians 1:15-20). He will VIVIFY ALL (I Corinthians 15:20-28). He will SUBJECT ALL to Himself (Philippians 2:5-11). And finally God will BECOME ALL IN ALL (I Corinthians 15:26-28). This is truly good news, especially for the millions of believers who have been told by church authorities that their deceased "unsaved" loved ones will suffer, or are already suffering, forever.

Paul explained to Timothy how the knowledge of the True God was to be passed on: "And what things you hear from me through many witnesses, these commit to faithful men, who shall be competent to teach others also" (II Timothy 2:2). Knowledge of the True God has been passed down that way, generation to generation, from Paul's time. Over many years, it has been passed down to me. This book is my means of fulfilling a calling to teach what I have learned about the True God. It explains how the True God, over the course of five eons, brings His creation to perfection, reconciles all, and becomes All in all of His creations. In the eyes of the Deity Who is Spirit, Light and Love, a cleansed and perfect universe is the only fitting result and reward for the sacrifice Christ has made. And all of this teaching accords with the Sacred Scriptures, portraying the very essence of them.

But how is it that so many people today have not even heard of the True God? In chapter seven of Mark and chapter twenty-three of Matthew, Jesus powerfully demonstrated how the ruling scribes and Pharisees of His day invalidated the Word of God by reliance instead upon their own doctrines and traditions. That tendency among "spiritual" leaders has, if anything, become worse. As the most characteristic sin of today, it is at the root of all religion—the essence of all error, the cause of sectarianism, and the mother of creeds and confusion. It should be comforting to know that the word "religion" appears so seldom in the Scriptures. Never is it applied to believers in Christ by God or an apostle or anyone else in sympathy with them. It never occurs in Paul's epistles which contain the special truth for today.

In the next three chapters, we will take a brief look at exactly how Christian "religion" hides the character of the True God, and then in the balance of this book, examine His true purpose in detail.

Chapter III

MISTRANSLATION—A CLOAK OF DECEPTION

The Purity of Scripture

The Sacred Scriptures are very different from other ancient writings. They make the claim throughout that they are the inspired word of the One, True Creator God. The Scriptures are not merely a grouping of religious instructions and moral principles in mystical language, but more important, a consistent, systematic disclosure of an explicit purpose which has been in operation since the dawn of time. From Genesis to Revelation, we are encouraged to believe God's Word, retain it in its purity, and ignore the so-called wisdom of men that contradicts it. Here are a few of these admonitions:

Ye shall not add unto the word which I command you, neither shall ye diminish ought from it . . . (Deuteronomy 4:2).

Every word of God is pure: he is a shield unto them that put their trust in him.
Add thou not unto his words, lest he reprove thee, and thou be found a liar (Proverbs 30:5-6).

Forever, O LORD, thy word is settled in heaven (Psalms 119:89).

Trust in the LORD with all thine heart; and lean not unto thine own understanding (Proverbs 3:5).

There is no wisdom nor understanding nor counsel against the LORD (Proverbs 21:30).

The Lord knows the reasonings of the wise, that they are vain (I Corinthians 3:20).

I am testifying to everyone who is hearing the words of the prophecy of this scroll: If ever anyone may be appending to them, God shall be appending to him the calamities written in this scroll (Revelation 22:18).

These words are not really so profound, but rather simple common sense. If the True God desires to communicate His nature, will, and purpose to His creations, we must allow Him to do it in His Own words. He has chosen His words more carefully than any other author: "The words of the LORD are pure words: as silver tried in a furnace of earth, purified seven times" (Psalms 12:6). Since words are the clothes in which thoughts are dressed, it follows that His thinking cannot become truly a part of our thinking if we alter His words to suit ourselves, or give the wisdom of created beings a higher place than the wisdom of the Creator Himself.

Bible versus Scripture

"All scripture is inspired by God, and is beneficial for teaching . . ." (II Timothy 3:16). Not all Bibles or all translations are inspired of God, but all Scripture. The Scriptures were not inspired in English, but in Hebrew and Greek. If we cannot read and understand these ancient languages, an accurate and consistent translation of the Sacred Texts into English becomes the most important factor in our quest for scriptural truth. The most prevalent deception throughout Christendom is the assumption that the translations of the Scriptures, particularly the revered King James Version (KJV), are inspired and therefore infallible. Because of this, many people are reluctant to accept any truth that is an obvious part of the original Hebrew or Greek Scriptures, but is not in their Bible. Of course this would not be a problem if the King James Version were an accurate, consistent translation of the ancient texts. But is it such? Absolutely not. The King James Version does not match the original manuscripts in many vital respects. The original Hebrew and Greek manuscripts have been added to, and taken away from throughout the text of this so-called "Authorized Version."

Soul and Judgment

Let me give you some examples. *Psuche*, for instance, always means soul each of the 113 times it appears in the original Greek. It never means life (which is *zoe*), or mind (which is *nous*), or heart (which is *kardia*). And yet, the King James scholars saw fit to mistranslate *psuche* into English 40 times as life, 3 times as mind, and 2 times as heart. God, by His Spirit, established the divine Greek vocabulary. The way He uses the words in that language is the way we are to understand them, and it is axiomatic that God chooses His words with utmost precision. Thus each of these 45 mistranslations of *psuche* mocks God, tainting and tarnishing His carefully chosen expressions of truth.

Another example is the Greek word *krisis*. *Krisis* means judgment or judging, the process of carrying out a judgment, or setting things right. This is what it always means in its 49 appearances in the Greek manuscripts. Although the King James scholars translated it correctly as judgment 41 times, they translated it incorrectly as accusation 2 times, as condemnation 3 times, and as damnation 3 times. Judgment is not the same as accusation or condemnation or damnation. In fact, there is no word in the Greek Scriptures that can be correctly translated as damnation. God did not express the concept of damnation when he "breathed out" His Word through His apostles and prophets—but yet it appears in the revered "Authorized Version." It is a forbidden addition to the Word of God.

Foundation and Disruption

Sometimes the King James scholars made the mistake of translating two different Greek words by the same English word. They translated both *themelios* and *katabole* as foundation, and yet in Greek these words are very close to being opposite in meaning. *Themelios* does, indeed, mean foundation in Greek, as in "the solid foundation (*themelios*) of God stands" (II Timothy 2:19), and "For other foundation (*themelios*) can no one lay beside that which is laid, which is Jesus Christ" (I Corinthians 3:11). But *katabole* does not mean foundation. *Kata* means down, and it comes into English in such words as cataclysm and catastrophe. *Bole* means casting or throwing. Together they mean down-casting. The whole word comes into English as catabolism which means "the breaking down of complex bodies."

There is no way that *katabole* is any kind of a foundation, and yet it is translated as such in the KJV ten times as in "the foundation of the world" (Ephesians 1:4). *Katabole* is in reality a disruption and is translated that way throughout the accurate and consistent Concordant

17

Literal New Testament (CV). The phrase "foundation of the world" in Ephesians 1:4 and elsewhere should read "the disruption of the world." Reading the KJV, you would never know that there occurred such a thing as the "disruption." And yet we are going to see in chapter ten that this concept is crucial to our understanding of God's purpose in creation, for the disruption of the world was the time—before Adam and Eve were created—that evil, by God's Own Hand, entered the universe.

The Restoration of the Earth in Six Days

Here's an example of mistranslation from the Hebrew Scriptures which relates to the hidden "disruption." We read in the KJV in Genesis 1:2, right after God created "the heaven and the earth," that "the earth was without form, and void; and darkness was upon the face of the deep." Did God create the earth that way? No. That passage should read, "Yet the earth **became** a chaos and vacant, and darkness was on the surface of the submerged chaos" (CV). If the Hebrew verb were *eue*, was would be an accurate translation; but it is *eie*, the causative form of BE which means become. This causative form (*eie*) appears more than 20 times in chapter one of Genesis alone, and everywhere denotes a change, and not mere existence. A concordant rendering of Isaiah 45:18 also shows that God did not create the earth "without form and void":

For thus says Yahweh, Creator of the heavens,
He is the God Who formed the earth and made it.
He established it.
Not a waste did He create it.
To be indwelt did He form it.

The earth was not created as "a chaos and vacant" but **became** that way as a result of "the disruption of the world" described in the Greek Scriptures. God thus did not create the earth in six days as is universally taught, but in that amount of time He *restored* the disrupted earth. Many important truths like these are hidden by multiple mistranslations.

The Myth of Lucifer and His Fall

Here's another example from the Hebrew Scriptures. Isaiah 14:12 in the KJV reads, "How art thou fallen from heaven, O Lucifer, son of the morning! how are thou cut down to the ground, which didst weaken the nations." This is the only reference to a being known as "Lucifer" in the entire KJV. Is it a valid translation? No. The Hebrew word translated as Lucifer is the very same word that the translators rendered "howl" in Zechariah 11:2. In slightly different forms it is found 10 times in Isaiah, and it is always rendered *howl* (13:6; 15:2,3; 16:7; 23:1, 6, 14; 52:5; 65:14). The name Lucifer is a man-made invention, and has no place in the Sacred Scriptures. The beginning of Isaiah 14:12 should read as it does in the Concordant Version: "How you have fallen from the heavens! Howl, son of the dawn." This chapter of Isaiah refers to the demise of the "king of Babylon" (v. 4), who is a "man" (v. 16), and not the spirit-being Satan.

This mistranslation helps foster the myth that Satan was created a good angel but later became prideful and "fell," somehow deciding to be evil on his own. The Scriptures relate that Satan was created purposefully as an evil being. "And I [God], I created the ruiner to harm" (Isaiah 54:16), and "[T]he Adversary . . . was a man-killer from the beginning" (John 8:44). From the myth that Satan was created "perfect" but "fell," follows the myth that Adam and Eve were made "perfect" but "fell." Evil and sin then become things outside of, and foreign to God's purpose—strange interlopers He did not want in His universe—instead of what they truly are: instruments under His complete control fashioned to achieve His ultimate purpose.

Evangels and Ecclesias

Let me introduce you to a very strange piece of educated inconsistency. The King James scholars translated the Greek word *eu anggelistes* (well-messenger) as evangelist, the word *eu anggelizo* (well-messagize) as evangelize, but then instead of translating the noun *eu anggelion* (well-message) as evangel, they translated it as gospel. The English word gospel has nothing to do with a "well-message" or "good news." It derives from a combination of the words god (small g) and spell. We will see the irony in this mistranslation in chapter five as we find that much of Christendom is under a kind of spell from some little god.

Perhaps you have seen a preacher wave his Bible (usually the KJV) from the pulpit and refer to "this gospel," as if the Sacred Scriptures contain one such "gospel." The contemporary usage of this word obscures the fact that there are two separate evangels, for two different groups of people in the Scriptures. One is the *evangel of the kingdom* which Jesus and His apostles preached to Jews and converts to Judaism only. It pertains to Israel as the "bride of the Lambkin" and her place in the coming **terrestrial** millennial kingdom. The other one is the *evangel of the grace of God* which pertains to the *"ecclesia* which is the body of Christ," and to the **celestial** destiny of this body of believers. An *ecclesia* is simply "a called out body." It is translated as church in the KJV, but since church has come to mean so many different things, including a building, the Concordant Version transliterates the Greek word *ecclesia* directly into English with its original meaning intact. The apostle Paul was himself "called out" to preach the evangel of the grace of God to individuals within the Gentile nations. In all the Scriptures, only he proclaims the evangel of the grace of God. And as he is the chosen "apostle to the nations," it is the truth for today.

There is a huge difference in these evangels, so much in fact that Paul reminded Timothy to "correctly cut the word of truth" (II Timothy 2:15); that is, understand which Scriptures pertain to Israel, and which to the nations. Many of the doctrinal problems in Christendom today come from mixing these two very distinct messages of good news into a contradictory, jumbled mess.

Believers Despoiled of the Truth

The above are just a few of hundreds of examples of the adulteration of the Word of God by the King James translators. By mistranslating Hebrew and Greek words, these men added to and subtracted from the Sacred Scriptures simultaneously. Each mistranslation is an addition which, at the same time, takes away, or covers, the true meaning. Paul wrote, "Beware that no one shall be despoiling you through philosophy and empty seduction, in accord with human tradition, in accord with the elements of the world, and not in accord with Christ, for in Him the entire complement of the Deity is dwelling bodily" (Colossians 2:8-9). The word despoiling in that passage means a robbing, a looting. Little by little, mistranslation by mistranslation, the truth has been stolen and replaced with profane prattlings and myths (I Timothy 4:7, 6:20). Many mistranslations have been systematized into a pattern of deception and fashioned into inviolable, but unscriptural creeds. Christendom thus presents to its followers a very different god with a very different purpose than the True God of the Scriptures.

The New Age Attraction

With their man-made doctrines, particularly those of Hell and eternal torment, the leaders of Christendom are driving millions of truth-seekers into the New Age movement. Offering a seemingly positive and hopeful explanation of existence and human destiny, this combination of warmed-over Hinduism and humanism makes more sense to many people than Orthodox Christian teachings. And well it should. But it is not true. Like all spiritual imitations in this present eon, the New Age philosophy has its origin at the Tower of Babel and the idea that man can save himself. I cannot fault anyone for looking away from Orthodox Christendom for a better god. But the secret to finding the True God is not to look away from the creeds of orthodoxy that are based on the mistranslations, traditions and philosophies of men, but beneath them, to the Sacred Scriptures in their purest form.

Think of each mistranslation as a dark thread. These threads have been woven together into a kind of pall, or cloak, which covers the truth beneath them. We will examine the fabric of that deceptive cloak in the next two chapters; then, we're going to pull it off. And as we do, "out of darkness light shall be shining" (II Corinthians 4:6).

A Spirit of Sanity

If you embrace a healthy skepticism about the God of Christendom, you should be able to jump right into this book. Whether you believe the Scriptures or not, at least you will have a better idea of what they truly say.

It will be more difficult for you if creedal Christendom has been a big part of your life; that is, if, over the years you have been systematically "in-[man's]doctrine-ated." Many of the things that you have been taught and have perhaps even been teaching to others will be challenged and shown to be out of line with the Scriptures. That's not always easy to accept. It took me a long time to understand what I now present in this book. It was difficult for me to untangle all of the false preaching I had heard, to sort out which doctrines are scriptural and which are not, and to gain an understanding of when the Scriptures are literal and when figurative. Let me suggest that you hang on to God and His Christ and do your best to let go of denominational teachings for now. If you are part of the body of Christ, no matter what denomination, you have nothing to fear from what you will learn in the chapters ahead, for God has given you "not a spirit of timidity, but of power and of love and of sanity" (II Timothy 1:7).

If I were you, whether skeptic or believer, I know what I'd be wondering first of all—what about that place of everlasting torment called Hell? Isn't that supposed to be part of the Sacred Scriptures? Let's move on to the next chapter and find out.

Chapter IV

HELL—A DOCTRINE OF DEMONS

Hel

When people today say, "I believe in Hell," they are essentially affirming their faith in Hel—the Norse queen of the underworld and her far-flung realm of weeping and wailing from whence she takes her name. While Hel appears throughout the King James Version and other translations, she has no place at all in the Sacred Scriptures.

Hell is the mistranslation of not simply of one, or of two, but of three different Greek words. The first is *hades*, the equivalent of the Hebrew *sheol*. They both mean "the unseen" or "the imperceptible." Hades is not an actual place, but rather a figurative condition of the human soul after death. The second is *Gehenna*. This is a valley just below Jerusalem. The garbage of the city and the corpses of criminals were thrown there to be devoured by constantly burning fires and ever multiplying worms. The bodies of the rebels will lie there during the millennial eon when Christ sets up His throne in Jerusalem, a warning spectacle for all who behold them (Isaiah 66:24). The third, *Tartarus*, is mentioned only once in the Scriptures (II Peter 2:4), as the place where sinning messengers (or "angels") are kept "to be reserved unto judgment." The KJV gives the name of the Norse goddess of the underworld indiscriminately to all three of these.

It is the human soul that supposedly suffers in Hel's eternal torture chambers, so let's search the Scriptures and see what they say the soul is, and what actually happens to it at death.

The account of man's creation in chapter two of Genesis reveals that we are made of two elements—soil and spirit—and that through this combination we become a third thing, what each of us is—a living soul. We find in verse seven that God is forming "the human of soil from the ground, and He is blowing into his nostrils the breath of the living, and becoming is the human a living soul." Soil and spirit are two. They alone, without any addition compose man. The soul is not a third and different element. It is the result of the union of soil and spirit, and without this union, the soul cannot be found.

The death of a human teaches us the same thing in reverse. As surprising as it may seem to many, death is not a new or unknown condition but a return. Man's body is soil and returns to it (Gen. 3:19). Man's spirit returns to God who gave it (Ecclesiastes 12:7). But what of the soul? The Hebrew Scriptures say it returns to a figurative "place" called *sheol*; the Greek Scriptures, to a figurative "place" called *hades*. Both words mean "the unperceived," or "the imperceptible." But it is not really a place for the soul, but a condition of it. Once spirit and body part in death, the soul essentially disappears, returning to the imperceptible whence it came (Psa. 9:17 and Acts 2: 27, 31). Neither man as a whole, nor any part of him enters a new, unknown condition at death, but all returns to the state from which it emerged when life was imparted. Literally, at death, the soul ceases to exist, because its two parts, body and spirit, separate.

By way of analogy, let's look at the composition of salt. As the soul is composed of two components, body and spirit, so salt is composed of two elements, sodium and chloride. Before we bring these two elements together, the salt does not exist except as a *potential* combination of these elements. Though the salt has the potential for existence, it is as yet imperceptible. So long as its two elements remain uncombined, we can say that the salt remains in the realm of the imperceptible. But then, when we bring the two elements together, sodium and chloride, under the right conditions, they form the third thing—salt. The salt, in a sense, becomes alive, real to the senses.

Now let's reverse the process. When we chemically separate the sodium from the chloride, the salt ceases to exist. In a sense it dies, returning to the realm of the imperceptible where it came from. We can bring the salt out of death and back into life by recombining the elements. So also our heavenly Father is able to bring us from death in the realm of the imperceptible to resurrection life with Him by combining our spirits, which upon death go to His keeping, with new and immortal bodies of His creation.

Note that when Jesus expired, He did not commend His soul to God, but rather He said, "Father, into Thy hands am I committing My spirit"

(Luke 23:46). The same is true of Stephen, the first martyr: "And they pelted Stephen with stones, while he is invoking and saying, 'Lord Jesus, receive my spirit!'" (Acts 7:59). Commending our souls to God upon death does not make sense because the "destination" of the soul is the realm of the imperceptible. It is our spirits which return to God for His safe-keeping.

The soul is the seat of our consciousness and sensations. It is our soul—our spirit operating in conjunction with our body—that perceives and feels. Soul is physical sensation, not spiritual life, for which it is usually mistaken. A soulish man likes the pleasures produced by eating and drinking and all other agreeable and delightful sensations, rather than the intangible experiences of the spirit. Soul and spirit are vastly different. They are never used synonymously in the Scriptures as they often are in theology and popular usage.

Without our spirit, our body is dead and feels nothing. Without a body, the spirit has no means of perceiving. We had no consciousness before God imparted life to us; and, since death is a return to the pre-life state, we would expect that there is no consciousness or sensation in death either. The Scriptures bear this out, teaching that the dead are unconscious, asleep, and oblivious until resurrection:

For in death there is no remembrance of Thee: In Sheol who shall give Thee thanks? (Psalms 6:5).

Whatsover thy hand findeth to do, do it with all thy might; for there is no work, nor device, nor knowledge, nor wisdom, in Sheol, wither thou goest (Ecclesiastes 9:10).

Look! answer me, Yahweh, my God! Illuminate my eyes, lest I should sleep in death (Psalms 13:3).

His spirit will pass forth, he will return to his ground. In that day his reflections perish (Psalms 146:4).

For the living know that they will die, Yet the dead know nothing whatever, And there is no further hire for them, For their remembrance is forgotten (Ecclesiastes 9:5).

Paradise

Throughout creed-ridden Christendom, the theologians and gospelizers teach that humans don't really "die" when they die but instead pass into a conscious intermediate state, either of bliss or of torment. To the question, "Where do people go when they die?", a prominent religious leader answered in one of his books, "As I understand the Bible, at death those who are Christians go to be with the Lord, to a place of bliss called paradise. Those who are not Christians go to a place of suffering and torment called hell." For many scriptural reasons this simply cannot be true—no matter how widely it is currently believed. First, as we have seen, there is no consciousness in death. The soul, the seat of sensation and perception, returns to "the imperceptible," essentially disappearing. The soul in death is not able to experience bliss or torment.

Second, paradise does not yet exist. Paradise is the terrestrial part of the "new heaven and new earth" described in chapters twenty-one and twenty-two of Revelation. Revelation 2:7 asserts that the "log of life" will be there "in the center of the paradise of God." It appears that the entire "new earth" will comprise this paradise. And as we shall see, it is a place for redeemed Israel, "the bride, the wife of the Lambkin" (Revelation 21:9), and not a specific place for that group of believers in Christ "which is his Body" whose destiny is not terrestrial but celestial (Ephesians 1:23).

And a third reason that Christians do not go to paradise at the time of their death is this: right now, Christ, by virtue of His resurrection from the dead "alone has immortality" (I Tim. 6:16). The myth that Christians go to paradise when they die contradicts this truth, asserting instead that millions now have immortality, when in fact they are dead. If death for the believers is but the entrance into a fuller, freer life of blessedness, then what need of a resurrection? Christendom's denial that death is actually what it is—the very opposite of life—also denies the possibility of resurrection. To make alive that which already has life should not call forth much effort. Yet resurrection is set forth as the mightiest exhibition of God's great power. And throughout the Scriptures it is insisted that it is resurrection from the dead, and not from some other life-form.

A Misplaced Comma

Where did the myth that death is but another form of life come from? A misplaced comma in the King James Version lies at the root of that misconception. In Luke 23:43, the KJV punctuates the words of Jesus to the thief on the cross this way, "Verily I say unto thee, Today shalt thou be with me in paradise," instead of, "Verily I say unto thee today, Thou shalt be with me in paradise." And so wise men reason from this mistake that if the thief died and immediately went to paradise, so then must we. And they reason so because a translator, a man, decided to put the comma before today instead of after it.

In the oldest extant Greek manuscripts—the Sinaiticus, Vaticanus, and Alexandrinus—all of the letters are uppercase Greek, there is no division between words, and there are no quotation marks, commas or other kind of punctuation. The division into verses is not part of the inspired original but was added to facilitate referencing. The original Greek of the above passage looks like this:

ΚΑΙΕΙΠΕΝΤΑΥΤΩΟΙΗCΟΥCΑΜΗΝCΟΙΛΕΓΩ
CΗΜΕΡΟΝΜΕΤΕΜΟΥΕCΗΕΝΤΩΠΑΡΑΔΕΙCΩ

Word-for-word, it reads, "And said to him the Jesus Amen to you I am saying today with me you will be in the park." In the Concordant Version it reads, "And Jesus said to him, 'Verily, to you am I saying today, with Me shall you be in paradise.'" And indeed the thief shall be with the Lord in paradise—after the resurrection of the just, and after the creation of the new earth which is yet to come. But right now, the thief on the cross is dead—sleeping, oblivious.

The idea of the thief joining Jesus in paradise that day was an impossibility, for that was the very day Jesus died. His spirit returned to God who gave it; His soul went to *sheol* or *hades*, the realm of the imperceptible; and His human body would have decomposed and returned to the soil had it not been ordained from above that His body should not see decay. If believing humans consciously experience paradise; that is, another life-form, when then die, then resurrection from the dead means little or nothing. And yet it is a central teaching, if not the central teaching, of the Greek Scriptures.

The placing of a comma before "today" instead of after it was a big mistake by the King James translators, and should be an object lesson in the dangers of putting one's trust in scholars or scholarship rather than in God and His Word.

Hel's Papa

How did Hel, the Norse goddess of the underworld, get into the Bible? First of all, we've seen that the term Hel, or Hell, misrepresents the words *sheol* and *hades*, both of which mean "the imperceptible," a figurative place of sleep, unconsciousness and oblivion. Hell, on the other hand, is a mythical world of darkness and pain. There, according to Norse legend, in a castle filled with the venom of serpents, sinners suffer torment while the dragon Nidhoggr sucks their bodies. Hell, then, in the Bible, is a perversion of truth, a false expression. It is closely related to the Norse verb *hylja*, meaning "to cover or to hide." We read in a first century letter to Timothy from Paul: "Now the spirit is saying explicitly, that in subsequent eras some will be withdrawing from the faith, giving heed to deceiving spirits and the teachings of demons, in the hypocrisy of false expressions . . ." (I Timothy 4:1, 2).

We have a false expression. Is there a demon involved? A deceiving spirit? Yes is the answer to both questions. Queen Hel's father is a terrible demon named Loki. It is said that he is the Mischief Maker of the gods and the first father of lies, a living shame to everyone, mortal and divine. He has a talent and skill in slyness that leaves everybody else far behind, knowing a trick for all occasions. He is known as the Forger of Evil, the Sly God, and the Slanderer.

It is indeed sly of him to slip his evil daughter and her realm into Bible translations when no such person or place is mentioned in the original Scriptures. He indeed encourages and forges evil: Hitler, Queen Mary, and many others tortured their enemies, reasoning that they were infidels, doomed to eternal punishment in Hell anyhow. And Loki has indeed effectually concocted the greatest slander against the character of the Supreme and Purposeful God of Love, presenting Him instead as a vicious and vindictive brute. Has a more vile and momentous trick ever been played upon Christians? And all this is accomplished through the insertion of just one simple and vexatious word meaning at its root "to cover or to hide." This is the spirit of deception at work. And it is a powerful spirit, indeed. The sorry truth is that Christendom has become so thoroughly deluded with the pagan ideas of death and Hell that it is practically impossible to get believers to consider the subject as it really is in the Scriptures.

The Scriptures do not teach a conscious intermediate state between death and resurrection. Neither do they teach that there is a place now in existence where the wicked dead are in torment. Furthermore, the passages referring to future judgment of unbelievers give positive statements that in the just judgment of God, all will be paid, or judged, in accord with their acts. In no instance is everlasting punishment or eternal torment so much as hinted at in the Scriptures in their purity. The pagan idea of Hell should never have been allowed to defile the pages of holy writ. There is no word in all the original Scriptures—Hebrew or Greek—which carries the significance of Hell according to the ideas taught and believed in Christendom today. Such teachings have been forced into the Bible through heathen dogmas and false translations, and on these orthodoxy depends to propagate the error. Worst of all, by this teaching, they have blotted the character of the True God of Love and Light.

The operation of the deceitful, the demonic, and the hypocrisy of false expressions helped finagle Hel into creedal Christendom. These same operations, united with the hoary traditions of religious men, have done even more damage by putting most denominations under a mysterious yet sanctified spell. Let's take a look at it.

Chapter V

THE RIDDLE, THE TABOO, AND THE THREAT

Manufacturing a Different Greatest Commandment

MARK 12:28-31
King James Version

And one of the scribes came, and having heard them reasoning together, and perceiving that he had answered them well, asked him, Which is the first commandment of all?

And Jesus answered him, THE FIRST OF ALL THE COMMANDMENTS IS, HEAR, O ISRAEL: THE LORD OUR GOD IS ONE LORD:

And thou shalt love the Lord thy God with all thy heart, and with all thy soul, and with all thy mind, and with all thy strength: this is the first commandment.

And the second is like, namely this, Thou shalt love thy neighbor as thyself. There is none other commandment greater than these.

Concordant Version

And, approaching, one of the scribes, hearing them discussing, having perceived that He answered them ideally, inquires of Him, "What is the foremost precept of all?" Jesus answered him that "THE FOREMOST PRECEPT OF ALL IS: HEAR, ISRAEL! THE LORD OUR GOD IS ONE LORD. And, you shall be loving the Lord your God out of your whole heart, and out of your whole soul, and out of your whole comprehension, and out of your whole strength. This is the foremost precept. And the second is like it: 'You shall be loving your associate as yourself.' Now greater than these is no other precept."

Whether we call it a commandment or a precept, or say that it is first or foremost, we get back to this as the basis of truth and faith: *the Lord our God is one Lord.* Men would never dream of trying to change the greatest commandment, the foremost precept, would they? In the minds of millions, belief in a mysterious Trinity has long ago replaced it.

If belief in the Trinity simply means belief in God the Father, the Son of God, and the operation of God's Spirit through Christ, I would have to say that, although the term Trinity appears nowhere in Scripture, I do believe in what the word stands for. But that is not what the Trinity doctrine is about. It is something very different. It asserts as fundamental truth that God is three coeternal, coequal persons each of whom is God and yet the teaching insists that there are not three Gods, but only one. Trinitarians refer to these three persons as God the Father, God the Son, and God the Holy Spirit. The phrase "God the Father" appears often in Scripture but nowhere in it do we find the terms "God the Son" or "God the Holy Spirit." The orthodox refer to God the Father as the "First Person of the Trinity;" God the Son as the "Second Person of the Trinity;" and God the Holy Ghost as the "Third person of the Trinity." Yet no language like this shows up anywhere in God's Word either. Like the term Hell, they are "false expressions."

I have had denominationalists say to me, "Son of God or God the Son, what's the big deal? We all know who we are talking about. It's just a matter of semantics." Is it just an insignificant matter of semantics? Let us do the same thing with the name of a person that the orthodox do with "God" and see if it amounts to a big deal or not. Let's assume that a million dollar check is to be presented to you, the "son of Richard." Why not just have the check made out to "Richard the son?" They are both the same person, right? Wrong. The "son of Richard" and "Richard the son" are completely different people. If you are the "son of Richard," your name might be Bill or Ed. Do you want that million-dollar check made out to "Richard the son"? I think not, because "Richard the son" is unmistakably somebody else. So also is theology's "God the Son" a completely different being than the Son of God!

In II Timothy 1:13 Paul wrote to Timothy, "Have a pattern of sound words, which you hear from me, in faith and love which are in Christ Jesus." Timothy never heard from Paul expressions such as "God the Son, God the Holy Spirit, trinity in unity, unity in trinity, coequal, coeternal," etc. They are not part of a "pattern [literally stencil] of sound words." They are not part of the Sacred Scriptures.

The question remains, how did these unscriptural expressions and the three persons they represent come into being?

The Three Incomprehensible Persons

Most denominational Christians were taught about the Trinity as children in Sunday School. Those who accept the doctrine usually have no idea where it came from because their teachers did not take the time to find out themselves, but just accepted it as a revered tradition and passed it on as such. If believers understood its origin, what it actually states, and the seriousness of contradicting the "foremost precept" of Scripture, they most probably would not believe it at all.

Philosophers dreamed up the doctrine of the Trinity over a period of about 300 years. The man who introduced the idea of co-equality of deities was named Athanagoras. He philosophized in the Greek marketplace at the foot of the Acropolis in Athens—beneath the pagan temple of Athena. Other philosophers developed his concept until the latter part of the 5th century A. D., when it was codified and adopted by the Roman Catholic Church as the Athanasian Creed. The Lutheran Church split from Rome, but kept this creed as part of its articles of faith. About 90 percent of today's Pentecostal, Evangelical, and mainstream Protestant sects accept its essentials as truth. As you read, try to pick out the scriptural expressions in it if you can:

ATHANASIAN CREED

Whoever will be saved: before all things it is necessary that he hold the Catholic Faith. Unless he keep this Faith whole and undefiled, without doubt he shall perish everlastingly.

And the Catholic Faith is this: we worship one God in Trinity, and Trinity in Unity, neither confounding the Persons, nor dividing the Substance. For there is one Person of the Father, another of the Son, another of the Holy Ghost. But the Godhead of the Father, of the Son, and of the Holy Ghost is all one: the Glory co-equal, the Majesty co-eternal. Such as the Father is, such is the Son, and such is the Holy Ghost. The Father uncreated, the Son uncreated, and the Holy Ghost uncreated. The Father incomprehensible, the Son incomprehensible, and the Holy Ghost incomprehensible. The Father eternal, the Son eternal, and the Holy Ghost eternal. And yet they are not three eternal, but one Eternal. As also there are not three incomprehensibles, nor three uncreated, but one Uncreated and one Incomprehensible. So likewise the Father is almighty, the Son almighty, and the Holy Ghost almighty; and yet they are not three almighties, but one Almighty. So the Father is God, the Son is God, and the

Holy Ghost is God; and yet they are not three gods, but one God. So likewise the Father is Lord, the Son Lord and the Holy Ghost Lord; and yet not three lords, but one Lord. *For like as we are compelled by the Christian truth to acknowledge every Person by Himself to be God and Lord, so we are forbidden by the Catholic religion to say, there are three gods or three lords.*

The Father is made of none, neither created nor begotten. The Son is of the Father alone, not made, nor created, but begotten. The Holy Ghost is of the Father and of the Son, neither made, nor created nor begotten, but proceeding. So there is one Father, not three Fathers, one Son, not three Sons, one Holy Ghost, not three Holy Ghosts.

And in this Trinity none is before or after the other; none is the greater or less than another; but the whole three Persons are co-eternal together, and co-equal; so that in all things the Unity in Trinity, and the Trinity in Unity is to be worshipped. *He therefore that will be saved must thus think of the Trinity.*

Furthermore, it is necessary to everlasting salvation that he also believe rightly in the Incarnation of our Lord Jesus Christ. For the right Faith is, that we believe and confess that our Lord Jesus Christ, the Son of God, is God and Man: God, of the Substance of the Father, begotten before the worlds: and Man, of the Substance of His mother, born in the world: Perfect God and perfect Man: of a reasonable soul and human flesh subsisting: equal to the Father, as touching His Godhead, and inferior to the Father, as touching His Manhood. Who although He be God and Man, yet He is not two, but one Christ: One, not by conversion of the Godhead into flesh, but by the taking of the Manhood into God. One altogether is Jesus Christ, not by confusion of Substance, but by unity of Person. For as the reasonable soul and flesh is one man, so God and Man is one Christ. He suffered for our salvation, descended into hell, rose again the third day from the dead. He ascended into heaven, sitteth at the right hand of the Father, God Almighty, from whence He shall come to judge the living and the dead. At his coming all men shall rise again with their bodies and shall give account for their own works. They that have done good shall go to life everlasting, and they that have done evil into everlasting fire.

This is the Catholic Faith. Unless a man believe it faithfully, he cannot be saved.

The Athanasian Creed has a cold and sinister spirit to it. You may have noted that it is made up of three parts: a riddle, a taboo, and a threat. The riddle: how can one be three and three be one? The obvious and true answer to the riddle is that one is *not* three and three is *not* one. Then comes the taboo. After having had three gods and three lords described to you in detail, you are *forbidden* to think or say that there are three ¹⁾ or three lords. In spite of what you've just been told, you must think and say that there is only one god and only one lord. Then comes the threat: unless you accept the riddle of the one and the three as an unsolvable mystery and respect the taboo against thinking about it and its implications, you can't be saved. The great "mystery of the trinity" turns out to be pure hocus-pocus dominocus; that is, nonsense intended to cloak deception pertaining to the Lord.

We can sum up the entire creed very simply:

> **Three is one, and one is three**
> **Believe what we teach, or burn for eternity.**

Were you able to find any Scripture in this creed? Except for a few minor phrases, the Word of God is virtually absent from it. When thoughts cannot be expressed in the language of inspiration, it should open our eyes to the fact that we are out of line with God.

Some violate the taboo against thinking about the three and the one, and go on to attempt their own solution to this man-made riddle. One notable gospelizer has written "[T]here are three separate and distinct persons—each one having His own personal spirit Body, personal soul, and personal Spirit . . . You can think of God the Father, God the Son, and God the Holy Ghost as three different persons exactly as you would think of any three other people—their 'oneness' pertaining strictly to their being one in purpose, design, and desire . . . In heaven we will see all three members of the Godhead: God the Father, God the Son, and God the Holy Ghost." This is outright tritheism—three gods. And this is where anyone who breaks the Athanasian taboo, and tries to solve the riddle, must honestly wind up.

Those who accept the taboo against examining the idea that three is the same as one, on the other hand, must either chalk it off as an incomprehensible "mystery" or defy common sense as they grasp for unusual ways to explain how three can be one and one can be three. I was riding down the highway earlier this year listening to a trinitarian preacher out of Texas. He thundered out that the three "co-equal, co-eternal persons" he worships are like a pretzel with three holes. That's right: *a pretzel with three holes*! His amplitude was unconvincing. I had trouble picturing the Infinite, Almighty, Invisible Spirit God which "the heaven and heaven of heavens cannot contain" as a brittle biscuit formed into twisted rings, glazed and salted. Doubtlessly oblivious to the import of his words, the preacher offered to his Christian radio audience a ludicrous graven image of God when the Scriptures say there is but One

Image worthy of human worship—Jesus Christ, the "Image of the Invisible God" (Colossians 1:15).

Note the phrase in the creed, "the Father incomprehensible, the Son incomprehensible, the Holy Ghost incomprehensible." The Son of God is the Image of God, the Mediator of God and mankind, and the Way to the Father—the One Whose purpose it is to reveal the Father to us. If the Son of God is incomprehensible, we would do better worshipping the sun, the moon or oak trees. And if everything about the Father is incomprehensible, Paul was wasting his time when he prayed that the Father "may be giving you a spirit of wisdom and revelation in the realization of Him, the eyes of your heart having been *enlightened* . . ." (Ephesians 1:17, 18).

But it so happened that in the early 5th century, A.D., the Trinity doctrine, an absurdity spawned by a spirit inimical to growing in the knowledge of God, became the foundation of Christendom. This hopeless enigma successfully barricaded the road to truth, and the *Dark Ages* followed.

Note also the phrase in the creed, "the Son uncreated." Theology's own King James Version even contradicts this. In Revelation 3:14, the Son of God describes Himself as "the beginning of the creation of God." We will go into more detail about this later, but right now let's just take His word for it.

The Athanasian Creed says, in essence, that if you do not agree to, and believe in something that it is impossible to understand, you cannot be saved. And even if you believe in this incomprehensible thing, it may not be enough because, as you may have noticed, the creed ties salvation directly to works. God's marvelous grace to us is utterly absent from this creed, as is thanksgiving to Him for His wondrous mercy and love.

That the doctrine of the Trinity lies outside the Sacred Scriptures and is a fanciful product of the minds of men is not disputed by the Catholic Encyclopedia. Under "Trinity, Holy" we read, "[W]hen one does speak of an unqualified Trinitarianism, one has moved from the period of Christian origins to, say, the last quadrant of the 4th century. It was only then that what might be called the definitive Trinitarian dogma 'one God in three Persons' became thoroughly assimilated into Christian life and thought," and "[T]he formula itself does not reflect the immediate consciousness of the period of origins; it was the product of 3 centuries of doctrinal development."

The Apostle Paul asserts that he was chosen "to complete the word of God" (Colossians 1:25), and his prison epistles, Colossians, Ephesians, and Philippians, did just that. How, then, can trinitarian ideas of Deity which had no place in Paul's writings be part of a true basis of faith? "Doctrinal development" of a completed revelation is unnecessary and false because it then becomes a prohibited addition to the Word of God. Everything we need to know and believe pertaining to God and His Christ can be found in the Scriptures.

Let me emphasize this point another way. Jesus said, "Not on bread alone shall man be living, but on every declaration going out through the mouth of God" (Matthew 4:4). "God the Son, God the Holy Spirit, trinity in unity, unity in trinity, coequal, coeternal," etc. are not declarations from the mouth of God. Why would you want your mind to ingest them? Why even consider them?

Let me again cite Paul's words to Timothy: "Beware that no one shall be despoiling you through philosophy and empty seduction, in accord with human tradition, in accord with the elements of the world, and not in accord with Christ, for in Him the entire complement of the Deity is dwelling bodily" (Colossians 2:8-9). All false doctrine comes to us via preceptors (idea men, philosophers, theologians) other than Christ. Note here that we are warned about philosophy and human tradition in the same passage in which it is expressed that the entire complement of Deity dwells in Christ bodily.

The nonsensical and unscriptural doctrines of the Athanasian Creed strike at the very heart of the greatest God-given commandment, or precept, that the Lord our God is one Lord. They have held Christendom spellbound for more than 1,500 years. With the hundreds of mistranslations and other man-made beliefs, it forms a big part of the dark cloak of deception covering the light.

As truth seekers, we have no use for that intricate cloak of deception. Now is the time to pull it off and believe the Sacred Scriptures in their purity. Since we are interested in the full scope of the Supreme Subjector's operations, a look into how He orders time is an excellent place to start.

Chapter VI

THE TRUE GOD'S TIME—THE EONS

"Eternity" Absent from the Sacred Scriptures

The Scriptures do not contain an adjective that can be properly translated as "everlasting" or "forever," and they never mention "eternity"—a concept which cannot be grasped by the human mind. Instead, the Scriptures reveal five definite time periods called eons (Greek = *aion*), long but measurable periods of time, through which the Subjector and Placer of all accomplishes His "purpose of the eons" (Ephesians 3:11), which also includes His purpose for humanity. Divine revelation is confined to the eonian times, so that mortals may comprehend it.

The Five Eons

This means that ultimately time is divided into three grand divisions, which are characterized in Scripture as "before the eons" (I Corinthians 2:7), "times eonian" (II Timothy 1:9) and "the consummation" (I Corinthians 15:24) which indicates the time after the conclusion of the eons. If we count all five of the eons in "times eonian," we have a total of seven secondary divisions—before the eons, the five eons, and the time after the conclusion of the eons. Such a division into three primary and seven secondary divisions is in perfect accord with both nature and revelation, for light itself is composed of three primary and seven secondary colors. Not only are there seven periods, but these are symmetrically grouped about that grand moral center of the universe— the cross of Christ Who is the Light of the world and the One through Whom and for Whom the eons were made.

As you can see by the chart on page 41, the eons commence with the beginning and close with the consummation, and are divided by four great judgments. The great cataclysm of Genesis 1:2—the disruption of the world-system—marks the boundary between the first and second eon. The deluge separates the second eon (Adam and Eve to Noah) from the one in which we live now. The coming Day of Indignation is the boundary between our times and the millennial eon. And the great white throne judgment separates the Millennium from the final eon, called the "eon of the eons" (Ephesians 3:21).

Eonian Clarity

You may be thinking that adding the word eon and its adjective counterpart eonian (*aionios*) to your scriptural vocabulary will cause a degree of consternation. Just the opposite is the case. When translated into English correctly (they are actually transliterated, or brought directly from the Greek), these words add great clarity, and clear up scores of contradictions that interfere with faith in the verity of God's Word. Let me give you some examples.

The So-called Unpardonable Sin

Probably most people under biblical influence have been either perplexed or distressed by this alarming passage in the King James Version:

And whosoever speaketh a word against the Son of man, it shall be forgiven him: but whosoever speaketh against the Holy Ghost, it shall not be forgiven him, neither in this world, neither in the world to come (Matthew 12:32).

Just why one particular sin is "unpardonable" has never been explained. The idea strains the spirit of a sound mind, to say the most charitable thing about it.

Some modern gospelizers have used this verse to put terror into their flocks, finding it a very convenient tool to frighten those they wish to persuade to seek salvation according to their formula.

THE PRE-EONIAN TIMES

The Beginning

FIRST EON
(Celestial Beings)

The Disruption

SECOND EON
(Adam and Eve to Noah)

The Deluge

TIMES   ### THE THIRD EON   **EONIAN**
(Man's Day)

The Day of Indignation

FOURTH EON
(The Millennium)

White Throne Judgment

THE FIFTH EON
(New Heavens and New Earth)

The Consummation

THE POST-EONIAN TIMES

They tell their hearers that if they do not respond promptly to an altar call, the Holy Ghost will cease to operate upon them for conversion, and in that case they will be eternally lost and doomed. Because they believe the Holy Ghost has ceased to plead with them to become a Christian, some so taught become certain that they are going to Hell. I know a young man who became a Christian as a teenager, but then began to drift away and dabble in white witchcraft. When he returned to his congregation, the preacher told him that by entertaining evil spirits, he had committed the unpardonable sin of blaspheming the Holy Ghost. From then on, the young man spent most of his waking hours searching through the KJV for a way out. This developed into a full-fledged obsessive-compulsive disorder requiring hospitalization and prolonged treatment. Many others have gone insane and become suicidal as a result of this entirely needless worry. Let's look at the Concordant translation of that passage:

"And whosoever may be saying a word against the Son of Mankind, it will be pardoned him, yet whoever may be saying against the holy spirit, it shall not be pardoned him, neither in this eon nor in that which is impending" (Matthew 12:32).

Now let's put it in context. Jesus is speaking here only to Jews pertaining to His coming kingdom. These words of His were fulfilled at the end of the book of Matthew and in Acts. All those who had spoken against Him as He taught the truth on this earth as the Son of Mankind were forgiven from the cross: "Father, forgive them, for they are not aware what they are doing" (Luke 23:34). But when, after His resurrection from the dead, He put His Spirit in His apostles at Pentecost, these same religious leaders ultimately rejected the truth for the second time. They were not forgiven. Jerusalem was destroyed and from that time through today, the kingdom expectation for Israel has been put on hold. These individuals did not receive forgiveness in this present eon, and they will not be part of the "resurrection of the just" at the beginning of the millennial eon, the eon "which is impending." They will not be made alive again until the end of the eons after the great white throne judgment.

Never, Forever, or For the Eon?

Let's look at John 8:51 in the KJV:

Verily, verily, I say unto you, if a man keep My saying, he shall never see death.

This is a real problem for, explain it as we may, those who kept His sayings have seen death. And what about John 10:28?

And I give unto [My sheep] eternal life; and they shall never perish, neither shall any man pluck them out of my hand.

What shall we do with these statements? Shall we refuse to believe Him Who is the Truth? Shall we convict Him of uttering self-contradictory statements that have not stood the test of time? These glaring discrepancies are eliminated immediately in the Concordant Version:

"**Verily, verily, I am saying to you, If ever anyone should be keeping My word, he should under no circumstances be beholding death for the eon**" **(John 8:51).**

"**And I am giving [my sheep] life eonian, and they should by no means be perishing for the eon, and no one shall be snatching them out of My hand**" **(John 10:28).**

Jesus is here referring to the immortal life conferred upon His sheep, not at the time He spoke those words, but at the beginning of the millennial eon, at the "resurrection of the just."

Now let's look at the parable of the fig tree in Matthew 21:19, KJV:

And when he saw a fig tree in the way, he came to it, and found nothing thereon, but leaves only, and said unto it, Let no fruit grow on thee henceforward for ever. And presently the fig tree withered away.

The fig tree represents Israel. Is Christ withdrawing the promises of God to Israel forever? Will His chosen people Israel never again bear spiritual fruit? Let's look at the Concordant version and find out:

And perceiving one fig tree on the roadside, He came to it and found nothing on it except leaves only. And He is saying to it, "No longer, by any means, may fruit be coming of you for the eon." And withered instantly is the fig tree.

Israel is withered, not forever, but only for the remainder of this present eon. In the oncoming millennial eon, Messiah will rule the entire earth from Jerusalem through her, and great indeed will be her fruit.

More Fabric for the Cloak of Deception

Many phrases concerning the eons appear in the Greek: "the coming eon" (Mark 10:30), "the oncoming eons" (Ephesians 2:7), "the conclusion of the eon" (Matthew 13:39), "for the eon" (John 4:14), "for the eons" (Luke 1:33), "for all the eons" (Jude 25), "for an eon" (Jude 13), "from the eon" (Acts 15:18), "from out of the eon" (John 9:32), "this eon" (Matthew 12:32), "that eon" (Luke 20:35), "before the eons" (I Corinthians 2:7), "before the entire eon" (Jude 25), the "eon of the eon" (Hebrews 1:8), "the eon of the eons" (Ephesians 3:21), and "the eons of the eons" (Romans 16:27). Every one of these expressions refers to specific, limited periods of time, and not to time without end.

How are eon, eons, and these related phrases translated in the KJV? To say discordantly is an understatement. We find an acceptable translation, "age," only twice. The rest are: "beginning of the world" (2), "course" (1), "eternal" (2), "ever" (2), "for ever" (27), "for ever and ever" (21), "for evermore" (3), "never" (7), "world" (32), "began" (1), "without end" (1) and "while the world standeth" (1). Eonian, the adjective counterpart of eon, or that which pertains to an eon, is translated: "eternal" (41), "everlasting" (25), "for ever" (1), and "the world began" (3).

Is there a word in English or any other language that sometimes means "age," sometimes means "world," and sometimes means "forever"? I don't know of any. The central meaning of each word in Scripture never changes however varied its usage, and neither do the number of words needed to express it in another language. It never takes on a sense that is expressed by another word. Each word in the original has only one central and basic significance. Otherwise, how could any sense at all be made out of God's Word? Everything would be subject to fallible human interpretation.

These KJV mistranslations of *aion*, *aionios* and related phrases, supply more fabric for the cloak of deception. By arbitrarily assigning very different meanings to *aion* and *aionios* from context to context, without recognizing a single, inherent meaning, the King James translators were able to introduce into the Bible their own beliefs in everlasting punishment, and more important, they obscured the fact that God is truly the living God Who is the Saviour of all mankind.

Without a knowledge of the eons, it is not possible to gain an understanding of God's "purpose of the eons." And likewise it is impossible to gain an understanding of God's purpose for humanity. Also, without knowing how things will be in the coming eons and at the consummation, it is impossible to know why things have been so unsatisfactory in the past, and sometimes seem so difficult now.

In the following chapters, we are going to look into God's eonian purpose, and then examine each of the eons and the judgments that divide them. This will lead us to the consummation, or end of the fifth and final eon when the Supreme Spirit of Light and Love reconciles all, and becomes All in all of His creations.

Chapter VII

THE PURPOSE OF THE EONS

O, the depth of the riches and the wisdom and the knowledge of God! How inscrutable are His judgments, and untraceable His ways! For, who knew the mind of the Lord? or, who became His advisor? or, who gives to Him first, and it will be repaid him? seeing that OUT OF HIM AND THROUGH HIM AND FOR HIM IS ALL: to Him be the glory for the eons! Amen! (Romans 11:33-36).

Out of Him and through Him and for Him is all. This is the most comprehensive statement that can be uttered. God is the source of all, the channel of all, and the object of all. The universe sprang out of Him, it has its course in Him, and He will be its ultimate. This settles all speculation as to the origin of all things. Creation is out of God, not out of nothing. This explains universal history. God is the One back of all the movements of mankind. This reveals the goal of all things. God is so guiding all His creatures that, eventually, He will become their All. If, in the above passage, God were speaking instead of Paul, God's great motto would read *Out of Me and through Me and for Me is all.* The Supreme Subjector binds together the origin with the object, and illuminates the beginning with the light of the conclusion. It is a closed circle.

Alfred Lord Tennyson concluded his *In Memoriam* writing of

That God, which ever lives and loves,
   One God, one law, one element,
   And one far-off divine event,
To which the whole creation moves.

This is the True God, the God of the Scriptures.

The Intimate Relation of God to All

Since All is out of God, there is, from the very start, an inseparable union between God the Creator and His creation. What we humans make with our hands has come into existence outside of ourselves and has no vital relationship to us. But with our offspring, who were in us and are out of us, we are in a close and living union. In fact, we could more accurately call our descendants our "outspring." And to us, they are the nearest, loveliest and best, our greatest and most valuable possessions. Because, at first, He carried all in Himself, God has established such a relationship with the universe. His ownership of all creation is not simply based upon His creation of it, but upon the fact that all was first included in Him. That is what gives Him the original title to the whole universe and all the creatures in it. He is the only true Owner of all that exists, and we are His outspring.

Out of Him and through Him and for Him is all. God's glorious and loving purpose is based and anchored here. God is Love and Light. This is His essence. *Out of Love and Light and through Love and Light and for Love and Light is all.* In this primeval revelation we find the necessity and root of the universal reconciliation of all. A clear conception of our Source and our intimate outspring from Him leaves room for no other conclusion.

The Yearning for Immortality

The full enjoyment of God's gifts is possible only in an imperishable life, for the earthly, disintegrating existence puts an end to every joy. Consciously or unconsciously, every human heart harbors a deep longing for an immortal life. Long before death started to reign over mankind, God's heart was filled with the desire to give all humanity such a life, through Christ, and so satisfy to the full this insistent yearning placed in us by the Subjector Himself.

This loving purpose, however, God concealed in Himself for a very long time—until the era came when the apostle Paul received the commission to reveal this secret. Clear and unmistakable are the promises of God to grant to all mankind unlimited life:

Our Saviour, God ... wills that ALL mankind be saved and come into a realization of the truth (I Timothy 2:4).

... according to the purpose of the One Who is operating ALL in accord with the counsel of His will ... (Ephesians 1:11).

We rely on the living God, Who is the Saviour of ALL mankind, especially of believers (I Timothy 4:10).

Consequently, then, as it was through one offense for ALL mankind for condemnation, thus also it is through one just award for ALL mankind for life's justifying. For even as, through the disobedience of the one man, the many were constituted sinners, thus also, through the obedience of the One, the many shall be constituted just (Romans 5:18, 19).

For God locks up ALL together in stubbornness, that He should be merciful to ALL (Romans 11:32).

... Making known to us the secret of His will ... to head up ALL in the Christ—both that in the heavens and that on the earth (Ephesians 1:9, 10).

... for in [Christ] the entire complement [of God] delights to dwell, and through Him to reconcile ALL to Him, whether those on the earth or those in the heavens (Colossians 1:20).

For even as, in Adam, ALL are dying, thus also, in Christ, shall ALL be vivified (I Corinthians 15:22).

[At the consummation Christ] subjects all to Him, that God may be ALL in ALL (I Corinthians 15:28).

These Scriptures show that the complete purpose of God in creating a universe of individual beings, both spiritual and physical, with faculties to comprehend Himself, is that He might eventually give life to all and be All in all. Toward this end He has provided a Mediator of God and mankind, Christ Jesus, Who gives Himself a correspondent Ransom for ALL (I Timothy 2:5). For as in Adam ALL are dying, so in Christ shall ALL be vivified. Here certainly is a marvelous opportunity to recognize the scope of God's purpose. Few will question that in Adam, ALL must die, or are dying. But when we read that, in Christ ALL shall be made alive, or vivified (given life beyond the reach of death), we reason that this must be limited only to the saved. But let us recognize that it is the same ALL! This passage could be written like this:

As in Adam		are dying
	ALL	
In Christ, shall		be vivified

In Adam ALL are dying through no choice of their own, and so, in Christ, this same ALL will be made alive, also through no choice of their own. Christ died for all so that all who die may be made alive in Him! What a transcendent revelation this is! God's will concerns all, His purpose includes all, and His goal is to be All in all! These are the facts which underlie His counsels and His dealings with His creatures, and which will result in His ultimate glory, and our immortality.

The original inclusion of all in God is so all-embracing that no creature can claim any independent origin. This unassailable truth leads us to think of one unique and mighty being—Satan, the adversary of God. He also had his beginning in God. The disclosure of this, his origin, is of great significance, for it gives us the proper basis for a correct understanding of his career and activity, and provides the key for the solution of the problem of evil in the world.

Before the eons, before time as we know it, the True and Only Spirit God of Light and Love was All in Himself. Who can even imagine the scene? God alone, abiding in glorious grandeur. Spirit, with nothing but Himself in which to dwell; Light, with nothing outside Himself on which to shine; Love, but with nothing, nothing whatever, to lavish itself upon.

Somewhere back there, All in Himself, God conceived His wonderful purpose. He chose to manifest His Love and Light through creation and willed ultimately to become All in all of His creations. God the Father, the Subjector and Placer of all, determined to accomplish this in the course of five eons. When these eons are completed, He will be All in all. All will know Him, all will enjoy immortality, and all will be happily subject to Him with boundless appreciation.

The True God conceived His grand purpose to become All in all before the eons. Hebrews 1:2 speaks of God's Son "Whom He appoints enjoyer of the allotment of ALL, through Whom He also makes the eons." But Who is this Son of God, the Christ, and where did He come from?

Chapter VIII

GOD'S CREATIVE ORIGINAL

We are now ready to see how our great God begins His creation with the Son of His Love. In Colossians, the epistle that unfolds His highest glories, He is called "the Firstborn of all creation." God thus speaks of His Son as a firstborn and as a creation. In Revelation 3:14, He is called "God's creative Original." Perhaps no saint would dare to invent such statements. But it is God Himself Who reveals to us Christ's place and tells us of His beginning.

Traditional theology is at great variance with the scriptural testimony of God concerning His Son. On their own, the theologians of Christendom have developed a doctrine to accord with the false teaching of the three mysterious co-equal, co-eternal persons. Christ, they say, is "eternally begotten." This expression is both contradictory and absurd, making it essentially incomprehensible. It thus fits well with the three incomprehensible persons of the Athanasian Creed.

The description of Christ as the "eternally begotten Son" eclipses His dignities and denies in a veiled way His divine Sonship. If the Son has existed eternally, like His Father, then He should not be a Son at all, but another God Himself, a co-equal and co-eternal *brother* of the other God, putting two Gods in the place of the One and only invisible Father God Who is manifest to us through His Son. Those who believe this doctrine should abandon the vain reasonings of men, open their own King James Bibles, and read Revelation 3:14 again. As we noted earlier, Christ describes Himself there as "the beginning of the creation of God." The translation is not exact, but close enough.

I worship, perhaps as you do, Jesus as God. But is Jesus Christ the ultimate Deity? No, He is not—but He is entitled to worship and praise as if He were. This seems at first to be an inconsistency, but it is not. You will see what I mean as we examine the scriptural relationship between God the Father and His Christ. As we do, we want to keep in mind that invisibility is one of the essentials of absolute Deity. God the Father is Spirit. He pervades the universe as the One Omnipotent, Omnipresent, Invisible, Creative and Loving Spirit. King Solomon wrote of Him:

> "Behold, I his son am building a House for the Name of Yahweh my Elohim to sanctify it to Him for fuming incense of spices before Him, for the continuous bread in array, and for the morning and the evening ascent approaches on sabbaths, on new moons and on appointed festivals of Yahweh our Elohim; for the eon this will be upon Israel. The House that I am building shall be great, for our God is greater than all the gods. Yet who could retain vigor to build Him a House, since the heavens and the heavens of the heavens cannot contain Him? And who am I that I should build Him a House save to fume incense before Him?" (II Chronicles 2: 4-6).

In God "we are living and moving and are" (Acts 17:28), and although He is "not far from each one of us" (Acts 17:27), not one of us has ever seen Him. He is absolutely invisible, not merely in relation to our present powers (I Timothy 1:17). This is important, if we wish to appreciate the part that Christ plays in His revelation.

Paul wrote, "Blessed be the God and Father of our Lord Jesus Christ" (Ephesians 1:3). Ultimate Deity does not have a God or a Father, and Jesus has a God Who is His Father. Consider these Scriptures also: "The Father is loving the Son and has given all into His hand" (John 3:35), "And, approaching, Jesus speaks to them saying, 'Given to me was all authority in heaven and on earth'" (Matthew 28:18). Ultimate Deity cannot be given authority by another. Therefore, Jesus, to whom all power has been given, cannot be Ultimate Deity. Consider also that Jesus is the Christ, the Anointed One. Ultimate Deity is not anointed. Ultimate Deity performs the anointing.

Jesus expressed His complete dependence on His God and Father when He said, "I cannot do anything of Myself" (John 5:30). God gave Christ the actual words He spoke, the very spirit with which He uttered them, the disciples whom He chose, His power, and His throne, and His glory. All are gifts to Him from God. Absolute Deity cannot receive such gifts, for He is Himself the Owner and Source of all. Jesus Christ will judge all unbelievers at the great white throne, but it is not His inherent right to do so. That belongs to absolute Deity. The Judgment of mankind is delegated to the Christ because of His humanity (John 5:22, 26, 27). All governmental authority is His as a gift also (Matthew 28:18, John 17:2). The Lord God will give Him the throne of His father David in the coming millennial eon (Luke 1:32). All glories that are His now and in the future come to Him from the Father's hand (John 17:22, 24; I Peter 1:21).

God the Father, the Supreme, knows no Deity above Himself. The Son continually acknowledges that He has a God. Is Christ then, some lesser God? No, He is not. Let's look at three things Jesus said of Himself to gain some understanding:

"**The Father is greater than I** " **(John 14:28)**
"**I and the Father, We are One**" **(John 10:30)**.
"**He who has seen Me has seen the Father**" **(John 14:9)**

How can all three of these statements be true? They can be if Jesus is the Image of the invisible God, the very One Who unfolds Him, and is the Radiance of God's Glory. And Jesus Christ is all of these:

. . . [G]iving thanks to the Father, Who makes you competent for a part of the allotment of the saints, in light, Who rescues us out of the jurisdiction of Darkness, and transports us into the kingdom of the Son of His love, in Whom we are having the deliverance, the pardon of sins, *Who is the Image of the invisible God* **. . . (Colossians 1: 12-14).**

God no one has ever seen. The only-begotten God, Who is in the bosom of the Father, He unfolds Him (John 1:18).

By many portions and many modes, of old, God, speaking to the fathers in the prophets, in the last of these days speaks to us in a Son, Whom He appoints enjoyer of the allotment of all, through whom He also makes the eons; Who, being the Effulgence *[Radiance]* **of His glory and Emblem of His assumption . . . (Hebrews 1: 1-3).**

As the Image of the invisible God, Jesus can say in truth that the Father is greater than He. As the One Who unfolds, or reveals, the True God, Jesus can say in truth that He and the Father are One. And, as the very Radiance of God's glory, Jesus can say in truth that if we have seen Him, we have seen the Father Who is otherwise absolutely invisible.

We humans can send one another photographs and watch ourselves and others on video. These images show only a part of our outer self, and are cold, lifeless, and two-dimensional. But, in Christ, God has given us a picture of Himself that is a living likeness, and, at the same time, He is the Way which leads us to God the Father. Through Christ, the Supreme Invisible Spirit becomes perceptible to His creatures. So perfectly does He picture the Deity that the Scriptures often call Him God, just as we speak of a photograph or a television image as if it were the one pictured.

Jesus Christ is described in the Greek manuscripts as the *Logos*. *Logos* is translated as word, but it means much more. It is the complete expression of a thought referring to a whole account. Here is John 1:1-3 and 14 with logos translated as expression instead of word:

In the beginning was the Expression, and the Expression was toward God, and God was the Expression. This was in the beginning toward God. All came into being through it, and apart from it not even one thing came into being which has come into being ... And the Expression became flesh and tabernacles among us, and we gaze at His glory, a glory as of an only-begotten from the Father, full of grace and truth.

God the Father created the eons and us through Jesus Christ, His Expression, Radiance, and Image. All things were created by the Invisible and Almighty God, through and for His visible Image, Radiance and Expression, Jesus Christ.

The Scriptures describe Jesus as God the Father's Complement: "... for in Him [Christ] the entire complement [of God the Father] delights to dwell," and "For in Him the entire complement of the Deity is dwelling bodily" (Colossians 1;19, 2:9-10).

A complement is that which fills up or completes, that which is required to supply a deficiency. God the Father is invisible. God the Father, in all His majesty, glory, power, and omnipresence is essentially incomprehensible to our limited minds. These are His deficiencies in relation to us. Jesus fills the deficiency by making Him visible to us. He is "the Image of the Invisible God." Jesus is God's Expression—the One through Whom He makes Himself known to us.

Colossians 2:9 is the only place in the Sacred Scriptures where the Greek word *Theotes*, meaning Deity, appears—"in Him the entire complement of the Deity (*Theotes*) is dwelling bodily." And in its context, it applies to God the Father alone: "For there is One God [the Father], and One Mediator of God and mankind, a Man, Christ Jesus" (I

Timothy 2:5). God the Father's full complement delights to dwell in Christ Jesus—ultimate Deity's very Image. It is this indwelling in Christ which makes the Infinite Spirit God that "the heaven and heaven of heavens cannot contain" and Who is "not far from each one of us" accessible to our understanding. As A. E. Knoch has written in his pamphlet *Christ and Deity*:

> So far as the revelation of Himself is concerned, the Deity needs a Complement, an Image, a Word, a Mediator, to make Himself known. Christ is the Complement Who fulfills these functions fully. The entire complement of the Deity dwells in Him in bodily form.
> Christ is not the complement of Himself. He is not engaged in revealing Himself. He acts for Another. That Other is termed "the Deity" in *contrast* with Christ. To say that the fullness of the Deity dwells in the Deity is not only unscriptural but an affront to the spirit of a sound mind. Outside of Christ there is a Deity. Inside of Him is the complement of this Deity. For the purpose of revelation, so far as our senses are concerned, Christ is that Deity. It is His function to show us the Father. Yet in so doing, He distinguishes Himself from His God, Who is here (Colossians 2:9) given a special term belonging to Himself alone. It will greatly aid us if we also confine the term "Deity" to the God of our Lord Jesus Christ, and refrain from applying it to our Lord ...
> All is *out of* God. All is *through* our Lord. Hence we read, "For us there is one God, the Father, out of Whom all is, and we for Him, and one Lord, Jesus Christ, through Whom all is, and we through Him" (I Corinthians 8:6). The contrast here is sharp and clear. It is the key to the part played by Christ in the course of the eons. Nothing *originates out* of Him or *consummates into* Him, though He is the Origin and Consummation. All comes *through* Him, from the beginning to the end. He is the Channel, not the Source or the Object of all things. It is a proof of divine inspiration that the Scriptures always maintain this point ...
> We are never said to come *out of* Christ, but *out of* God. Indeed, Christ asserts that He Himself came out of God (John 8:42). All is out of God (Romans 11:36). But God never deals with us except *through* His Anointed. Hence, while all is sourced in God the Father, all is channeled through the Son ...
> He is the only Way to the Father, the only means through Whom we may know God.

The highest glory of the Son of God is that He displays His Father to us; His Father is greater than He, and to do the will of His Father is His chief delight. But, occupying the unique place which is His, it becomes

His due to receive all the worship, gratitude and recognition which we owe to God, for Christ is God to us, as far as our perceptions are concerned, since it is in and through Him only that we can realize, appreciate and approach the Father. That is how I can say that I worship Jesus as God and yet recognize that He is not the Ultimate Deity. Yet, at the same time, I recognize that Jesus Christ, as the "Image of the Invisible God" is inseparable from our Heavenly Father. This is how I understand the foremost precept in all the Scriptures—the Lord our God is One Lord—and believe it. It's simple: "For there is one God [Who is *Spirit*], and one Mediator of God and mankind, a Man, Christ Jesus" (I Timothy 2: 5), and in that Man "the entire complement of the Deity is dwelling bodily" (Colossians 2:9).

If God's heart were not overflowing with a love that transcends all knowledge, He would doubtless be satisfied to be alone in His invisible existence. But His love yearns for fellowship with His intelligent beings who once were in Him, and who were created by Him. The desire of His heart is to bestow upon them His life, and grace them with His gifts, and bless them with His happiness, in order to enjoy the bliss of reciprocal love.

In the vastness of His affection, God has thought out the wonderful way by which He will attain this goal. He creates a Son in His image (Colossians 1:15), the radiance of His glory and emblem of His assumptions (Hebrews 1:3), Who has all His essential characteristics, and bears His likeness. It is by no means dishonoring to the Son to speak of Him as created. His likeness to God, as His Son, gives Him a much more desirable and practical place than if He had come out of eternity and were a second-rate Deity. As such He could never be the Mediator, because His mediatorial mission between God and His creatures is based on the truth that He proceeded from out of God. In a sense, the creation of Christ is the Supreme Invisible Subjector's begetting of His Own relation to His creation.

Now that we are acquainted with the One through Whom the Supreme Spirit made the eons, we can move on and see His purpose and place in each one, and in the awesome judgments which divide them. When we get to the end, to the consummation, we will look back and marvel at God's perfect means of becoming All in all His creations through His Christ, the Son of His love.

Chapter IX

THE FIRST EON—THE CELESTIALS

Created by the Elohim (God) were the heavens and the earth. Yet the earth became a chaos and vacant, and darkness was on the surface of the submerged chaos (Genesis 1: 1, 2).

These first two verses of Genesis span the entire first eon, whose length we do not know, from the beginning to the disruption.

After creating His visible Image, the Invisible, Supreme Subjector and Placer needed intelligent beings to be recipients of His revelation. We have no clue whatsoever as to when the creation of heavenly bodies or stars began, or when and with what kind of creatures these were populated. The only thing we do know is, that there was a wonderful world before our earth came into being.

The universe is full of life and has been since long before God created mankind. There are spirit beings with far greater powers than anything possessed by humans, and numerous beyond computation. Let us note what Nehemiah has to say:

You are He, Yahweh You alone. You Yourself have made the heavens, the heavens of the heavens and all their host, the earth and all that is on it, the seas and all that is in them. You are keeping all of them alive, and the host of the heavens are prostrating themselves before You (Nehemiah 9:6).

Nehemiah can ignore all the multitudes of earth in this picture; it is the host of heaven that is so important, hundreds of millions of them just "around the throne" of God (Revelation 5:11). There are probably billions or trillions of celestial beings, or more.

It helps us to remember that humanity is not the first, nor indeed the greatest, of God's creations. These are to be found in the heavens, where there are sovereignties and authorities and powers and lordships evidently controlling vast numbers of subjects (Ephesians 1:21, Colossians 1:16). These celestial beings existed before God created the earth. We know that because in Job 38:4, 7, God Himself asks: "Where wast thou when I laid the foundations of the earth . . . when the morning stars sang together, and all the sons of God shouted for joy?" This one short passage teaches us that God allowed celestial beings to look on when He called a new, marvelous masterpiece into existence; and these beings were able to appreciate the power and wisdom exhibited in it, and to rejoice.

God's dealings during this first eon are exclusively with these celestial creations. And this original, or first earth, God created to be inhabited (Isaiah 45:18). He created it in light, for He is Light, and darkness in Him there is none (I John 1:5). Above the earth was the first of three heavens as this earth was the first of three to come into existence over the course of the eons as described in the Scriptures. This first grand and glorious world was not marred by any discordance, any trace of rebellion, enmity, or sin.

The First World Not Perfect

Now some might think that this must have been a perfect world, enjoying a perfect revelation, and therefore capable of bringing the most perfect satisfaction to both God and the beings He made. But this was not so. All that His creatures were then able to see was a Creator of unlimited power and ability. His innermost heart remained hidden from them. They could know Him as the embodiment of might and grandeur, but how could they know Him as the embodiment of love without a background of enmity? They could not know good as long there was nothing with which to contrast it. The Deity they could grasp resembled the One Whom countless unbelievers, or heathen, admire in nature—the One Who makes the heavens appear to move around the earth, Who brings on the wind, the rain, the seasons, the fruit of the soil, and the lightning. These celestial creations could worship God's revelation, the Christ, only as a disclosure of these kinds of awe-inspiring creative powers and splendors. They could fear Him, but why should they love Him?

God knew another revelation was needed; needed for His own sake, for the sake of His Christ, and for the sake of His creatures. It was the revelation of evil. And thus this glorious and harmonious eon ended with a cataclysmic disruption.

Chapter X

THE DISRUPTION OF THE FIRST WORLD-SYSTEM

All is contrived by Ieue [the LORD] for His response, even the wicked one for the day of evil (Proverbs 16:4).

Former of light and creator of darkness,
Maker of good and creator of evil,
I, Yahweh Elohim, make all these things (Isaiah 45:7).

Behold! I, I created the artificer who blows into the
Fire of coal,
And brings forth and implement for his occupation.
And I, I created the ruiner to harm (Isaiah 54:16).

Between the first and second eons comes the disruption of the original, harmonious world-system and the imposition of darkness. We've seen in chapter three that disruption is mistranslated in the KJV as foundation. The Greek *katabolo* is nearly the opposite of a foundation, being in truth a down-casting.

We need to review those first two verses of Genesis for emphasis, contrasting the misleading King James version with the Concordant one:

**In the beginning God created the heaven and the earth.
And the earth was without form, and void; and darkness was upon the face of the deep. And the Spirit of God moved upon the face of the waters (KJV).**

Created by the Elohim were the heavens and the earth.
Yet the earth became a chaos and vacant, and darkness was on the surface of the submerged chaos (CV).

Common sense alone tells us that there is something very wrong with the King James translation. First, why would God create the earth without form and void? And since God is Light, why did He create it in darkness? Second, try to picture an earth without form. If you are an artist or have an artist friend, ask him or her to draw you a sketch of an earth without form, or an earth that is void. You can't picture it and you can't sketch it because it doesn't make any sense. Now picture an earth that has "become" a chaos and vacant. We can do that and even sketch one, and, most important, that translation agrees with the original Hebrew.

But why did the first earth become a chaos and vacant? This is the time of the introduction of evil power into the universe. Celestial rebellion and angelic enmity toward God ensue. The earth becomes "a chaos and vacant, and [as God's light is withdrawn] darkness [is] on the surface of the submerged chaos" (Genesis 1:2). Here we see a first reference to that jurisdiction of darkness later spoken of by both Jesus and Paul (Luke 22:53, Colossians 1:13). The whole evidence of the Scriptures regarding darkness is that it is a negative force, an evil related to sin. Thus are created "the spiritual forces of wickedness among the celestials," the sovereignties, the authorities, and world-mights of this darkness destined to oppose God, His Christ, and His people (Ephesians 6:12).

The First of Two Floods

At the conclusion of the disruption, the first of two great cataclysmic floods inundates the earth. We know this because at the very beginning of God's restoration of the down-cast earth, His Spirit vibrates over the surface of the water, and He says, "Flow together shall the water from under the heavens to one place, and appear shall the dry land" (Genesis 1:3, 9).

Since natural science cannot contradict the Scriptures in their purity, geologists would do well to consider the disruption and subsequent inundation. The great disorder in the earth's crust could only be the product of extremely violent upheaval. Only the disruption explains it. It is very possible that the first earth rotated harmoniously, and that its present tilt and wobble resulted from the disruption.

The Disruption in the Greek Scriptures

This disruption is referred to many times in the Greek Scriptures. So that we might know that Satan, evil, and darkness are always subservient to the ultimate purpose of God, Revelation 13:8 asserts that Christ is "the Lambkin slain from the disruption of the world." Figuratively, God neutralizes evil the moment it is created with the fore-ordained blood of Christ. The apostle Peter goes even further, letting us know that the blood of Christ is foreknown "before the disruption" (I Peter 1:20). Our Heavenly Father, the Subjector and Placer, would not have created evil had He not already prepared its perfect antidote in accord with His "purpose of the eons." In short, the slaying of the Lambkin was not a consequence of anything attributable to Satan, who will never be allowed to claim that he was able to change God's designs. It was not an improvisation to correct something that had gone awry in God's plans, but was an integral and predetermined feature in His purpose.

The fact that the Lambkin is slain "from the disruption" clearly identifies the sacrifice of Christ with the needs of the celestial beings, for the disruption of the world is the moment of scriptural recognition that there had indeed been rebellion among them, coming, as it did, before the creation (and sinning) of humanity. The arch-exponent of all evil, the Adversary of God's operations, Satan the deceiver, is a celestial himself, who has multitudes of followers. These all require the benefits of the blood of Christ's cross before reconciliation between God and them can be effected. Colossians 1:20 covers all in heaven as well as all on earth: ". . . and through Him to reconcile all to Him (making peace through the blood of His cross), through Him, whether those on the earth or those in the heavens."

Jesus said that the millennial kingdom of the Jews, yet to come, was made ready for them "from the disruption of the world" (Matthew 25:34). Without the operation of hostile powers during the evil eons, and the rule of Satan on this earth, how could God's chosen people appreciate the uncontested rule of Messiah for a thousand years?

God the Father chose those who believe in Him through Christ "before the disruption of the world" (Ephesians 1:4). This was a time when God's counsels were unchallenged and His love unquestioned.

This should solve all questions relating to "conditional salvation" and the significance of mankind's vaunted "free will." My salvation does not depend on me, and your salvation does not depend on you. What a relief! Our salvation was assured even before the eons came into existence. For it is "God . . . Who saves us and calls with a holy calling, not in accord with our acts, but in accord with His own purpose and the grace which is given us in Christ Jesus before times eonian . . ." (II Timothy 1:9). The theologians of Christendom tend to forget that the Supreme Subjector also has a free will, and a glorious purpose for all of humanity—neither of which can be countermanded by His created beings. He has selected some to be a part of His chosen people, Israel, the "bride of the Lambkin." He has selected some to belong to "the ecclesia which is [Christ's] body." And He has chosen to reconcile, justify, and glorify the rest at the end of the eons. Will you question His plan? Do you want some credit for believing and being good?

O man! who are you, to be sure, who are answering again to God? That which is molded will not protest to the molder, "Why do you make me thus?" Or has not the potter the right over the clay, out of the same kneading to make one vessel, indeed, for honor, yet one for dishonor? (Romans 9:20, 21).

The Ultimate Outcome of the Disruption

A great work can only be properly judged by its outcome. Every part of it, especially the preparations for it, must be seen in the light of the final effect. Only by a full realization of the results of God's dealings with the celestial beings, the earth and humanity, are we able to judge and appreciate His power and wisdom and love. If popular theology were correct and the great majority of earth's denizens were doomed to everlasting death or despair, then the creation of the earth, its chaos and partial readjustment, the introduction of sin and offense, the deluge, God's dealings with Israel, and the terrible judgments of the future—all the fearful suffering of mankind—will reveal the Creator and Subjector in the worst possible light as lacking power and wisdom and love.

But if we accept His own words as to the future, our estimate of Him will be the reverse of this. If all mankind will be saved (I Timothy 4:10), and justified (Romans 5:18), and reconciled (Colossians 1:20), and thus have been prepared by their suffering and sorrow to enjoy God's love endlessly, what a blessed boon will that be for them and for God! All will look back upon their brief burdens with thankful hearts and adore the One Who thus drew them to Himself.

His chosen ones, the saints, have the greatest incentive to praise God for the ruin that followed creation, for it has given them the greatest privilege that can come to a creature, to be God's ambassadors, to make Him known, not only to mankind, but to messengers in other realms, and to reign with Christ, until all God's creatures are brought back to Him in love and He is All in all. The chaos following creation was the initial preparation for God's great purpose to draw His creatures close to Himself, through their suffering, and the suffering of His Son for their sakes. Let us, then, not only admire His power and wisdom in creating the heavens and the earth, but also bless and adore Him for the subsequent disruption of them and their restoration in six days for the purpose of revealing His grace and His love.

The multifarious, marvelous wisdom involved in the creation of evil and the subsequent counterplay of forces is far beyond the imagination of man and infinitely higher than the dark devices of the evil spirit world. They are defeating their own purpose while opposing His, and He is accomplishing His intention through their opposition to His will.

Once we see the unparalleled wisdom of God in using these spirit forces to carry out His plan to reveal Himself and to bless His creatures everywhere, we lose all dread of the mighty spiritual powers that infest the darkness of this eon. Apart from Him, they are ferocious, fearful, destructive, devastating. In His hands they will work the well-being of man and win them for the worship of God.

Let us move on to the second eon. There, once the Supreme Subjector and Placer restores the disrupted earth in six days, an evil spirit force He created will cause Eve to eat of the tree, and in the following eon, bring about the crucifixion of the Son of God.

Chapter XI

THE SECOND EON—MANKIND

Thus far we have an almighty God Who is Spirit and therefore invisible to those He has made. We have His visible Image, the Christ, and we have a universe of suns and planets, with intelligent beings living in those realms, beings created for the purpose of receiving the revelation of God, in order that He should be satisfied through the response to it in their hearts. And, to activate this revelation, we have Satan, a being of incredible cunning, ability, and power, to whom God gives a stage, a platform, on which he demonstrates what he can do in opposition to God, and what his capacities will achieve apart from Him. This stage is the earth, on which he is allowed to display his true character. A fine object lesson for the hosts of heaven.

But this alone would not accomplish God's purpose in creating evil. Where would the revelation of God's heart come in? Where is the revelation of the unutterable superiority of Christ over every other being, not as the most high, but as the most worthy of all? Where is the revelation of the value of absolute dependence on God in contrast to Satan's career of self-will and elevation? What good would it do for the witnesses of his misrule, if the Adversary were permitted to go on eternally in his character, without his sin ever coming to a consummation, without bringing about his utter defeat and the triumph of good? This scenario would never lead to an adequate revelation of the depths of grace hidden in God and of the lengths that His love would go; nor of the depths of iniquity in Satan, and to what a climax evil could come. Something more was needed.

So God, in six days (Genesis 1:3-31), went about restoring the ruined earth for the scene of His crowning revelation. This called for circumstances in which Satan would have an opportunity to attack God, demonstrate all his antagonism toward God, and go to the incredible culmination of murdering the Representative of God. Then, when he believes that he has triumphed over God, he must discover that he has brought about his own complete and final defeat, as well as the glorious victory of the One he wished to destroy.

Satan could never touch the Christ existing in the form of God. In order that Christ may be challenged by Satan to mortal combat, the Son of God had to empty Himself of His divine majesty and take on a body adapted to this struggle, a body that could be hurt, broken, and sacrificed. As the first specimen of such a being, God created the first man, Adam.

What it must have meant to God when He formed this wonderful creature in His own image! Man had to be God-like to such an extent that the Christ could become a man without sacrificing His real status. Even in the glory, Christ is and always will be a Man. This one fact places man far above all the principalities and powers of the heavenly realms. Christ never took on their likeness, and God did not choose them to be the instruments of His crowning revelation to the rest of creation. Once we grasp that we were made in order that Christ could, in our form and likeness, reveal to the universe what God is, what He Himself is, and what Satan is, we can only raise our hands in adoration. Such a vision, once it dawns on us, is overwhelming. It is an answer to the question of our existence that surpasses in its marvelous grandeur all human explanations, as God's wisdom surpasses ours. But there it is, hidden in the Scriptures.

Let's review the first five verses of Genesis:

Created by the Elohim were the heavens and the earth.
Yet the earth became a chaos and vacant, and darkness was on the surface of the submerged chaos.
Yet the spirit of the Elohim is vibrating over the surface of the water. And saying is the Elohim, "Become light!" And it is becoming light. And seeing is the Elohim the light, that it is good. And separating is the Elohim between the light and the darkness. And calling is the Elohim the light "day," and the darkness He calls "night."

And coming is it to be evening and coming to be morning day one (Genesis 1:1-5).

These five verses of Genesis cover a lot of time. Verse one describes the beginning of the first eon. Verse two describes the end of that eon, the disruption of the cosmos and the introduction of sin, evil, and darkness into it. Verses three through five describe the beginning of God's restoration of the earth in six days that leads to the creation of Adam and Eve. This restoration of the earth and creation of mankind is the start of the second eon.

When we read "And it is becoming light," we are seeing the first signs of the dispersal of that deep spiritual darkness which surrounded the celestials as a result of their rebellion against God in that first eon, and of which the physical darkness that engulfed the earth was merely a sign and a token. And when we read down that first chapter of Genesis and see the restoration of the earth after the disarray caused by the disruption, when it became a chaos and vacant—when we read of vegetation reappearing and of animal life being created, we are, in fact, seeing the stage being set for Golgotha. The props are being prepared.

The vegetable, animal, and mineral kingdoms all were required to effect the events surrounding the crucifixion. The wood of the cross and the crown of thorns represent the vegetable kingdom. The nails which pierced the Victim's hands and feet represent the mineral kingdom. The thongs which lacerated His back represent the animal kingdom. (The animal kingdom also provided all the typical sacrifices in ancient Israel which, throughout the centuries, pointed to the real Sacrifice). Only the human element was missing, and this had to be a special creation, made in the image and likeness of God, in order that He, Who was His true Image and Likeness, might come in human form without ever losing that resemblance to God.

The Creation of Mankind

On the sixth day God creates living souls on the land, and also humanity. Here we reach the peak of God's six days of reconstructive work, and history moves forward to unfold that which God had planned before times eonian.

The evil of the disruption has not been fully eliminated, but light with its possibilities has been introduced, and so there is a partial respite from the ruin of creation, and God's world moves forward again under His ordering.

The Spirit of God the Father, through Christ, vibrates over the surface of the water, and restores the earth in six days. This is the second of three earths described in the Scriptures. He rearranges the heavens making this the second of three heavens described in the Scriptures. It is the earth on which, and the heaven under which we live today. We live on the second earth under the second heaven. The third earth and third heaven called "a new heaven and a new earth" (Revelation 21:1) do not come into existence until the end of the millennial eon

On the sixth day of this second eon, God the Father creates Adam and Eve in His Image and Likeness. God creates Adam's body "of soil from the ground," and brings his body to life by "blowing into his nostrils the breath of the living." This spirit, in living combination with the body, becomes "a living soul" (Genesis 2:7). Adam and Eve are created with a nature which accords with God, with a conscience that is good, except it be seared, but with flesh flawed by a propensity toward sin and rebellion because of its impending mortality.

God creates Adam and Eve with an ultimate objective in mind—an objective that is to be accomplished by Jesus Christ in the likeness of humanity. We learn in Colossians 1:20 that God purposes to reconcile all to Himself through Christ: "through Him to reconcile all to Him (making peace through the blood of His cross), through Him, whether those on the earth or those in the heavens." This necessitates the creation of a lower order of beings, mortals, through whom an incarnation of God's image and expression might suffer and die to effect, through love, this reconciliation. God brought humanity into being as a special and separate creation to be used by Him in rectifying the evil wrought by Satan among His prior celestial creation, and in restoring peace between Him and His whole universe. God placed Satan, the created Adversary of God and His Christ, in the guise of the serpent in Garden of Eden for the express purpose of tempting Eve, bringing sin and death into the world, and inaugurating human history and human destiny so that a Saviour might be born into it.

The First Judgment of Mankind

When the serpent misrepresents God to Eve, deceives her, and Adam joins in the transgression, God ordains that Adam and Eve and their progeny must experience death. The presence of sin, evil, and death begin to characterize human existence.

The first judgment is still in operation today. We should understand, not only the reason for it, but its object and its scope. It was not confined to Adam and Eve, but includes the race which springs from them, and which was in them when they first offended. We can look back and see ourselves there in a very practical way, for we are serving the sentence, even if we did not personally commit the offense. Many are embittered by this, and claim it is not just. They do not see that it was passed for Adam's sake, and for our benefit. Vindictive punishment breeds hate, but God's judgments, though bitterly hard to bear at times, are rooted in love, and will bear the blessed fruit of final Fatherly affection.

Man is banished from God in order to be brought back, like the Prodigal Son, after having experienced what it means to live without Him. The function of the alienated spirit world is to turn man's worship away from God to Satan. They organize mankind into great religious bodies that become powerful and seem to succeed in driving God out of the earth, and almost succeed in wiping His saints from its surface. But because God's love can be fully displayed only where enmity and hate have done their utmost against Him, and because this is the special function of the Adversary, he has really only done and will do that which must promote God's great plan.

Had Adam Not Sinned

How many have wished that Adam had not sinned! Some have even gone so far as to assert that they would not have done so if they had been in Adam's place! In this they are sadly mistaken, not only as to their conduct, but as to the desirability of Adam's sin. Even Adam, after he had eaten of the tree, and gained the knowledge of good and evil, would not have eaten, and it is most likely that he did not do so again. But, if we had no such knowledge, we all would have done the same. The knowledge of good is one of our most precious assets. What a dreary life we would live if we appreciated nothing that is given us, and were utterly devoid of thankfulness! A few spoiled children exhibit that kind of behavior, and are a trouble to themselves and a trial to others. A humanity with no appreciation for good might have resulted in endless misery, not only for the race, but for the Creator Himself.

How valuable, therefore, is the knowledge of evil! It may not be pleasant, or prized for itself, but it is the essential prelude to the enjoyment of good and the worship of the Supreme. Good, by itself, cannot be appreciated unless contrasted with evil.

As the prime purpose of creation is to draw forth the response of love from hearts overflowing with affection, so that, as Father, He becomes All in all, the Supreme Subjector introduced evil as a transitory, yet indispensable necessity for the accomplishment of His will. For this reason the Adversary was created and the tree was planted in Eden. And this explains the part played by the serpent. Evil leads to the appreciation of good.

Experience and Judgment

We need more than a theoretical knowledge of evil. The experience of evil humbles the human heart, and judgment must follow in order to clarify and emphasize the lesson. Therefore, following the first offense, God judged all who took part in the evil, and intensified rather than healed it, so as to give it full force. The need for judgment is evident, for all seek to evade their guilt by shifting the blame to another. The man accused the woman and the woman passed it on to the serpent. But none of the excuses were accepted, and each was judged in such a way as to impress upon them the knowledge of evil, so as to prepare them for final restoration and the enjoyment of the abundant blessings still in store for them. Then they will be able to give Him the praise and adoration that His heart desires.

We need not learn all we know of evil by suffering ourselves, for this also prepares us to perceive it in others, and to sympathize with them even if we are not ourselves involved. Many who are comparatively free from pain themselves have tasted enough of it to feel for others. Apart from this how could we apprehend the fearful sufferings of our Saviour which stir our heart to its depths, and move our lips to thankfulness and praise and worship? Is not the cross of Christ the greatest evil in the history of the universe? And yet it will bring about the greatest good.

Celestials Learn

Not only will mankind benefit by the evil introduced through Adam, but celestial beings also will profit by our experience. The long record of evil in the history of the human race, as chronicled in the Scriptures, culminating in the crucifixion of Christ, is their textbook, which will enable them, not only to apprehend His wisdom (Ephesians 3:10) but learn of His love, so that those that are estranged from God will be reconciled to Him (Colossians 1:20).

The Judgment of the Serpent

The serpent did not pass on the blame to anyone else but fulfilled the function for which it was created, like the Adversary that it represented. Nevertheless, for the sake of mankind it was necessary to put it in its proper place. Even to this day, most of us have an intuitive horror of serpents, but there is little intelligence as to the reason for this aversion. In contradicting the word of God, the serpent exalted itself, not only above all the animals and man, but also above its Creator. Eve should never have listened to it or acted on its word, but should have submitted to the Subjector and to her husband. Because it had usurped the highest place, God degrades the serpent to the lowest.

The Judgment of the Woman

Grief and groaning, specially suited to her functions in the perpetuation of the race, were allotted to the woman, corresponding to the part she played in the offense. So far as the record goes, she was not told to abstain from the fruit of the tree of the knowledge of good and evil by God, but by Adam. So she was subject to neither when she ate the forbidden fruit. Nothing is said before this as to her subjection to Adam, but now this is definitely asserted, since, in disobeying him, she also offended his Subjector. But this experience of evil is accompanied by a promise of restoration, through this very function. With her husband the race will be perpetuated until the Second Man, the last Adam (I Corinthians 15:45, 47), will bring about its restoration.

Man's place and his nature and his constitution were given him by God in order to carry out His grand purpose for the universe. Sin and its accompaniments, suffering and death, though they seem to thwart God's beneficent design, in reality are essential to its fulfillment, for they provide mankind with that realization of its own futility without God. This understanding must precede their subjection to Him.

Love and Grace

Love lacks a contrast for its display in a perfect environment. If the Supreme Subjector had not wrecked and ruined the earth in the beginning and all nature were pleasant and perfect as on the original earth, and if Adam had not introduced sin and dying and death, how little need would there be of God's intervention in the affairs of mankind! He would remain the unknown, the unloved Deity, unneeded, unwanted, and unappreciated by the creatures of His hand and heart, and without the affection which He craves, not only from mankind, but from the celestial hosts as well.

Above all other things there was need of sin, which would produce suffering and misery, so that there would be the need and the desire for a Saviour; as well as estrangement and enmity in human hearts, so that there could be reconciliation, and God could draw humanity closer to His heart than any of His other creatures. Such an outcome demands an imperfect environment to produce it.

The Supreme Subjector wishes to reveal His hand by making the first last and the last first (Luke 13:30). This will not only be so on the earth in the coming millennial kingdom, but in the universe as well. The dregs of the earth will become the highest among the celestials. His Son came down to the deepest depths of earth, and to the dreadful death of the cross, in order to be raised to the place supreme. So, also, the despised of this world will be made judges of messengers (I Corinthians 6:3). If God is to be All in all, it is necessary that He do all according to the counsel of His will even in the wicked eons when men act as a foil to show His all-conquering might. Estranged humanity on a disintegrating earth provides Him with just the opposition He needs.

God saw all that He had made and found it very good (Genesis 1:21). This is the divine viewpoint, with which we heartily agree. It seems to contradict the human aspect, which we have been considering. These two seem to differ because God looks at the intrinsic essence and the ultimate result, while we see nothing but the temporary outward appearance. When we consider the conclusion of the eons, even the evil eons are transformed into good by the result. For the great purpose of revealing God's wisdom and love, all the evil background is indispensable and effective, hence beneficial. But to shortsighted humans, who cannot see the sequel, it seems to be very bad indeed.

The Remainder of the Second Eon

After the description of the restoration of the earth, and the transgression of Eve and offense of Adam, we have only a scant outline of the rest of the second eon. The events of nearly two thousand years are condensed within little more than two chapters (Genesis 4:1 to 6:8).

Cain Kills Abel

In Genesis 4:3-8, we read of Adam's and Eve's youngest son, Cain, killing his younger brother Abel. Cain presented Yahweh with a sacrifice of his own choosing "from the fruit of the ground," displeasing God. Abel presented to God a blood sacrifice, prefiguring Christ's sacrifice, "from the firstlings of his flock." Cain became enraged that God rejected his sacrifice, despite the fact that God had provided an acceptable sin offering for him saying to Cain, ". . . at the opening [of your abode] a sin offering is reclining, and for you is its restoration. And you are rule over it" (Genesis 4:7). But Cain's anger at Abel could not be assuaged. He lured Cain to the field, and there murdered him.

God condemned Cain to be a rover and a wanderer in the earth, but Cain defied the will of God again by building and living in a city he named after his son, Enoch.

Prelude to the Deluge: The Seth-men Take the Cain-women

Eve bore another child to replace Abel. "And calling is she his name Seth, saying, 'For set for me has the Elohim another seed instead of Abel, for Cain kills him'" (Genesis 4:25). Seth's lineage is the one through which the ancestry of Christ is traced back to Adam and Eve. The number of humans grew:

And coming is it that humanity starts to be multitudinous on the surface of the ground, and daughters are born to them. And seeing are sons of God [Seth-men] the daughters of the human [Cain-women], that they are good, and taking are they for themselves wives of all whom they choose (Genesis 6:1-2).

The sons of God are not spirit-beings as some misinterpret this passage. They are men in the line of Seth who are taking the Cain-women, not as mere conquests, but as "wives."

In my books, *The Parthenon Code: Mankind's History in Marble* and *Noah in Ancient Greek Art*, I show that the ancient Greeks remembered this event, depicting the taking of the Cain-women by the Seth-men on the south side of the Parthenon, and on the temple of Apollo at Bassai. On both temples, the Cain-women are pictured as clinging desperately to an idol-image as they are being taken by the Seth-men.

The abducted Cain-women never abandoned their idolatry. In Genesis 6:4, just two verses after their abductions, we find the Cain-women becoming the defacto heads of the Seth families: ". . . coming are those who are the sons of God [Seth-men] to the daughters of the human [Cain-women], and they bear for them." The Seth-men failed to subject their wives to God, and the Cain-women raised their children to be idolators just like themselves. Thus, the taking of the Cain-women led to Godless offspring throughout the Seth families. And as a result:

. . . seeing is Yahweh Elohim that much is the evil of humanity in the earth, and every form of the devices of its heart is but evil all its days (Genesis 6:5).

God spoke to Noah:

"The era of the end of all human flesh is come before Me, for full is the earth with wrong because of their presence. Now behold Me ruining them with the earth" (Genesis 6:13).

In this ancient world of the second eon, from the disruption to the deluge, we discern a background that displays the bitter and hopeless evil of the human race when under the control of Adam and his sons. Not only did the first man who was born kill his brother, but the last generation became evil all its days. At the close of this eon, with the exception of Noah, who finds grace in the eyes of God (Genesis 6:8), the descendants of Adam do evil and fill the earth with wrong (Genesis 6:11). God's judgment is inevitable.

Chapter XII

THE DELUGE

On this day rent are all the springs of the vast submerged chaos, and the crevices of the heavens are opened, and coming is the downpour on the earth forty days and forty nights.

On this very day come Noah, and Shem, Ham, and Japheth, Noah's sons, and Noah's wife, and the three wives of his sons, with them, into the ark, they and every living animal for its from-kind, and every beast for its from-kind, and every moving animal moving on the earth for its from-kind, and every flyer for its from-kind, every bird of every wing. And coming are they to Noah into the ark, pair by pair, of all flesh, which has in it the spirit of the living. And those coming, male and female of all flesh, come as Alueim instructs him. And closing the ark is Ieue Alueim about him.

And coming is the deluge forty days and forty nights on the earth. And increasing are the waters, and lifting up the ark, and it is high above the earth. And having the mastery are the waters and they are increasing exceedingly on the earth, and going is the ark on the surface of the water. And the water has the mastery exceeding exceedingly on the earth. And covered are all the lofty mountains which are under the entire heavens. Fifteen cubits above has the water the mastery, and covered are all the mountains.

And expiring is all flesh moving on the earth, of flyer, and of beast, and of living animal, and of every roaming animal roaming on the earth, and every human. Everyone which has the breath of the spirit of the living in his nostrils, of all that were in the drained area, dies. And wiped off is every risen thing which was on the surface of all the ground, from human to beast, from moving animal to the flyer of the heavens. And being wiped are they from the earth. Yea, only Noah is remaining, and what is with him in the ark. And lofty are the waters on the earth a hundred and fifty days (Genesis 7:11-24).

Thus God brings a second flood upon the entire Earth, through which Noah and his family and many pairs of animals pass safely in the ark.

No Flesh-Eating Animals

During Adam and Eve's eon, animals were not carnivorous. Green herbage was the food of all land life, and for every flyer of the heavens, and for every moving animal on the land (Genesis 1:30). That this is by no means impossible is evident from the fact that it will be so again in the millennial eon (Isaiah 11:7). The present flesh-eating animals are abnormal, like much else that we mistakenly imagine to be natural. It would not be practical to take wild, carnivorous beasts into the ark, for they would devour all the rest. Man's control of the animals during the preceding eon was much greater than at present. Noah had to store a supply of all the food needed on the ark. This could not have included flesh.

The First Rain

The evil inhabitants of the earth must have been absolutely terrified when water began to fall from the sky, for from the time of Adam to Noah no rain had fallen on the earth. We read that "at that time Yahweh Elohim does not bring rain on the earth . . . Yet humidity is ascending from the earth and irrigates all the surface of the ground" (Genesis 2:5, 6). This ascending humidity made for a very different climate than we experience, with none of the extremes of moisture or drought, which makes some of the earth uninhabitable in this eon. This may have been one of the reasons for the long lives at that time. During the deluge, water came from below and above, and the two sources together were enough to cover all the land. The fact that there is enough water to cover the entire land surface of the earth even today to a depth of more than a mile, shows the possibility of a universal flood. The earth had been prepared beforehand for the deluge of water, just as it is now stored with fire for the future conflagration between the fourth and fifth eons.

The Suffocation of Evil Humanity

After forty days the waters reached their maximum, and remained so for a hundred and fifty days. This caused all that had *the breath of the spirit of the living* in their nostrils to expire. This is a notable and instructive expression, showing the relation of breath to life in the creatures on the surface of the earth. Humanity cannot live on food alone.

It needs air to breathe. The deluge did not kill by cutting off their food, but their air. It is here called the breath of the spirit of life. It is the spirit that gives life, through the breath. This is not only literally true, but a fine figure of the spirit of God, which gives real, divine life. The earth dwellers were already dead in the higher sense, so the deluge simply conformed their physical condition to their spiritual state. Had there been no deluge, mankind would have become so saturated with sin that it would have rotted away by a much more painful and prolonged death than drowning. By using the best family as a new start, they were saved much suffering.

The Raven and the Dove

Noah picked out a raven to scout the scene and see if the time had come to leave the ark. As it did not return, he sent out a dove. Are these not significant, as indicating what kind of world it was to be? The raven is black and eats anything, and could live on carrion. It was the first inhabitant of this world, and has had many human followers. It no longer needed the shelter of the ark, so did not return. The dove, however, could find no place to light and rest, so it comes back to the shelter of the ark. It is a symbol of peace and holy spirit (Matthew 3:16). So is the one who has the spirit and the peace it gives. There is no place for him to rest down here. Refuge can be found only in Christ.

Noah's Faith

Noah displayed a most public and persistent exhibition of faith. For a considerable period he was engaged in building a ship on dry land. If anyone should attempt this today, his sanity would be in serious doubt. Yet, in essence, believers in Christ are in the same boat. Because of their faith, as I Thessalonians 5:9 points out, they are not appointed to indignation, but to the procuring of salvation through our Lord Jesus Christ. We will not be saved by an ark from a watery deluge, but by being snatched away to meet the Lord in the air, and rising to realms celestial. That will be the signal for the outpouring, not of a flood of water, but of divine indignation, to prepare the earth for the next world.

We find Noah listed with Daniel and Job, as highest examples of mortal righteousness (Ezekiel 14:14). Our present race of humanity was given the best possible start by excluding all the men who were the cause of the deluge, from its line, and coming only through one who was graced with divine righteousness by faith. Noah, being a first-born son in the line of Seth, belonged to the "distinguished" of those days (Genesis 6:4). Not being in the line of Cain, which typifies insubjection, but a head in the line of Seth, which was subject to God, he was "flawless in his generations," and was chosen to start the new world, in which the great lesson of subjection would be further developed by a different method of enforcing it.

Noah Compared With Adam

When we compare Noah with Adam, we find a great advance. Adam was innocent, without the knowledge of good and evil, so that he failed at the very first test. But Noah was not only well-acquainted with evil, but had overcome it. Adam had walked with God in the midst of great goodness, but later hid from Him, and was driven from His presence. Noah lived in the midst of an evil generation, which was opposed to the Subjector. Nevertheless, he walked with God in the midst of it all. Noah condemned the world about him by building the ark when there was no indication of any deluge. He embodied a great advance, due to the knowledge of evil, as the inaugurator of the present world. It was commenced by a man of faith (Hebrews 11:7). He is like Adam in that he is the ancestor of us all.

In a very real sense, all mankind since the flood was not only in Adam in Eden, but also with Noah in the ark. All were saved with him from the waters of the deluge. This puts them in a dearer relation to the Subjector than those living in the previous eon. Then, He had *created* men and *made* them. In this eon, He has also *saved* them through a great cataclysm, which is a clear intimation of the future, when He will once more become the Saviour of all mankind, not in the ark, but in Christ (I Timothy 4:10). Not by creation, but through *salvation*, will the Father bring all under His beneficent and loving sway at the consummation.

Through his three sons, Noah not only commenced the present world in which nations and kings stage another failure, but, through Shem, he started one nation and one King, Christ Jesus, by which the world after ours will be a success in bringing humanity under the rule of the Supreme Subjector.

Chapter XIII

THE THIRD EON—MAN'S DAY

As this is the eon in which mankind crucifies the Son of God, it is called "the present wicked eon" (Galatians 1:4) and "man's day" (I Corinthians 4:3).

Human government commences after the deluge, when God, after again giving man his place over the animals by putting the fear and dread of him upon them, adds the new provision that whoever sheds man's blood, by man shall his blood be shed (Genesis 9:2-6).

This present world, from the deluge to the coming kingdom, introduces control by means of nations, or human government. Their superficial function is to govern well, but their underlying duty is to display their inability to rule ideally. We should be most lenient in our criticism of their acts, for they are quite helpless to subject those who are not subject to the Supreme Subjector.

Mankind is now given an opportunity to display its utter incompetence to rule. It is given free rein, so that all imaginable forms of government may be given an opportunity to exhibit their weaknesses and shortcomings.

The waters subside and God the Father blesses Noah and his sons Shem, Ham, and Japheth. He tells them, "Be fruitful and increase and fill the earth and subdue it" (Genesis 9:1).

Babylon is represented as the original center of human civilization after the Flood. This is where Noah's grandson, Cush, and his followers attempted to build the tower of Babel:

And saying are they, each man to his associate, "Prithee! Let us mold bricks and burn them with a burning." And coming is the brick to be their stone, and asphalt becomes their mortar.

And saying are they, "Prithee! Build will we for ourselves a city and a tower with its head in the heavens, and make for ourselves a name, lest we are scattering over the surface of the entire earth" (Genesis 11:3, 4).

But then God intervened and said,

"Behold! One people is it. And one lip is for them all. And this they started to do! And now nothing will be defended from them of that they will plan to do. Prithee! Descend will We, and there disintegrate their lip that they may not hear each man the lip of his associate" (Genesis 11:6, 7).

Thus God confounded their language and scattered them over the entire earth.

The tower of Babel was meant to procure renown for its builders, and serve as a center and bond of unity, so that none would think of leaving it. The text indicates that men intended to form a universal empire. Left to their own devices, Cush and his associates would have ushered in the climax of "man's day" way ahead of schedule. It is foreordained to come at the end of this eon. In "disintegrat(ing) their lip" God saw to it that mankind will not be united again in full force against Him until the end of the time of the Gentiles, when man's day reaches its awful climax in the worship of the False Prophet, Wild Beast, and Man of Lawlessness (Revelation 13). Mankind had to be scattered into different nations and languages so the God's plan could be fulfilled. A unified world left no place for God's Chosen Nation and People, Israel.

From Babylon also, Cush and his son, Nimrod, established the basis of all imitation religious systems, and this "secret of lawlessness" began to operate. It will culminate in the appearance of the "Man of Lawlessness" during the coming "Day of Indignation."

Abraham to the Christ

From chapter eight of Genesis through the writings of Paul, we learn about the workings of God during this eon. After the call of Abraham, His focus is on Israel. As we review the time from Abraham to Christ, please keep in mind that there is much, much more we could include, but for brevity's sake we include only what follows.

God calls Abraham and makes a promise to him: "And your seed shall tenant the gateway of its enemies, and blessed, in your seed, shall be all the nations of the earth, inasmuch as you hearken to My voice" (Genesis 22:18).

God renames Abraham's grandson, Jacob, meaning "supplanter" as Israel, meaning "he will rule as God" (Genesis 35:10). His twelve sons become the heads of the twelve tribes of Israel.

God, through Christ, establishes Israel as His chosen nation and people. Those of that nation who are redeemed during the course of the eons He considers as "the bride, the wife of the Lambkin" (Revelation 21:9).

Over and over again, the prophets of Israel predict the coming of the Messiah to rule over the nations of the entire earth from Jerusalem through His chosen people.

God delivers His people out of bondage in Egypt and gives the law to Moses. God purposes that Christ, His Expression, the Righteous One, should come in the flesh to fulfill the law (Exodus 20-23, Matthew 5:17).

God makes a special point to command the Israelites not to worship any graven image, for there is One and only One Image in the entire universe worthy of worship—Jesus Christ, the Image of the Invisible God (II Corinthians 4:4, John 20:28, Revelation 4:9-11).

Isaiah prophesies that God will rule from Israel through a Man born of the seed of David, and that this Man will rule the whole earth with "the club of His mouth" (Jeremiah 23:5, Isaiah 9:7, 11:1-5).

Isaiah writes that during the time of this earthly Kingdom ruled by Christ, "the wolf will sojourn with the he-lamb, And the leopard will recline with the kid" (Isaiah 11:6).

Ezekiel prophesies that the people of Israel will be scattered among the nations (Ezekiel 36:19).

Ezekiel prophesies that God will bring the scattered Israelites back to their homeland, and establish the center of His earthly kingdom there, through them. When this Kingdom comes, God will give His people a new heart and a new spirit (Ezekiel 36:24-26).

Isaiah promises "new heavens and a new earth," alluding to the final eon, the "eon of the eons," when God Himself will be the Light of the earth (Isaiah 65:17-18, 66:22-23, 60:19-20).

Zechariah predicts that Jesus will enter Jerusalem for the first time in humility, "riding on an ass, and on a colt, the foal of a she-ass" (Zechariah 9:9).

Isaiah and Zechariah allude to the millennial eon, predicting that Jesus will return to Jerusalem a second time in glory and power (Isaiah 2:2-4, Zechariah 14:4).

Isaiah prophesies that Israel will reject its Messiah and King (Isaiah 53).

Micah prophesies that the One who will rule Israel will be born in Bethlehem (Micah 5:2).

Grace and Truth

Jesus Christ is born in Bethlehem, the city of David (Matthew 2:1). Grace and truth come through Him (John 1:17).

John the Baptist announces that the kingdom is near as Jesus Christ begins His ministry to the Jews (Matthew 3:1-3).

John the Baptist identifies Jesus not simply as the One who takes away the sins of believers, but as the "Lamb of God Which is taking away the sin of the world!" (John 1:29).

The Messiah comes to redeem His people, Israel, be their King, and become the Saviour of the whole world. Christ, His apostles and disciples, including John the Baptist, preach the good news of the coming earthly kingdom (the evangel of the kingdom) to Jews and converts to Judaism only (Matthew 10:5-6).

In the Sermon on the Mount Jesus describes the values which will have force in His coming earthly Kingdom (Matthew 5:1-12).

Jesus teaches Nicodemus that repentance and baptismal regeneration are essential for entrance into the earthly kingdom. When Christ speaks to Him, He uses the plural "you" referring to Israel as a whole. Though a teacher of Israel, Nicodemus is ignorant of the fact that he and the entire nation must be "begotten anew" by God to enter the earthly Kingdom of Christ. He should have been familiar with Ezekiel 36:26-33. (John 3:1-12).

Jesus calls Judas Iscariot as one of His twelve apostles knowing full well that Judas will betray Him (John 13:21-26).

Jesus, through the parable of the rich man and Lazarus, prophesies that the Nation of Israel will reject Him a second time even after He is raised from the dead (Luke 16:20-31).

Jesus affirms that judgment will come on earth against unfaithful Israel and the unbelieving nations. He prophesies a foretaste of that greater judgment when He describes the destruction of the Temple and the nation of Israel, which came to pass under the Roman general Titus in 70 A. D. (Matthew 26:61).

Jesus prophesies a "great affliction" to come, at the end of the eon, worse than anything that has ever happened on Earth (Matthew 24:21).

Jesus speaks to the Jews of a "resurrection of life" and a "resurrection of judging" to come (John 5:29).

He warns that when the Jews perceive the "abomination of desolation" as declared through Daniel the prophet standing in the holy place, they should flee into the mountains (Matthew 24:15-18).

Knowing that He will be rejected by His people and must bear the shame of hanging on a pole, Christ gives the keys of the kingdom to Peter in preparation for the Pentecostal administration (Matthew 16:19).

One of Christ's own apostles betrays Him—after Satan enters into him, and the religious leaders of Israel, working with a reluctant Roman governor, cause Him to be crucified. But on the ultimate level, it is God Who causes this for, in accord with His purpose of the eons, the Supreme Subjector "desires to crush Him, And He causes Him to be wounded" (Isaiah 53:10).

Before dying and giving up His Spirit to His God and Father, He says, "It is accomplished." He dies "for our sakes" and for the sake of the "whole world also" (I John 2:2). What is required for the ultimate reconciliation of all takes place (Colossians 1:20).

After three days in the tomb, God the Father raises Jesus from the dead to immortal life. He thus becomes, "the Firstborn of the dead" (Revelation 1:5) and the "the Firstfruit of those who are reposing" (I Corinthians 15:20). He is seen by His apostles, and by a total of over five hundred witnesses (I Corinthians 15:6).

The Pentecostal Administration

At Pentecost, Peter, who has the keys of the kingdom, begins to preach the good news of the kingdom again. Proclaiming Jesus as Lord and Christ from the Scriptures, he preaches repentance and baptism to Jews and Jewish converts only. The apostles and believers receive spiritual gifts as evidence of "the powerful deeds of the impending [millennial] eon" (Hebrews 6:5).

That power does not continue. As we trace the exhibition of that power through the Book of Acts, we see that as the kingdom expectation vanishes, power also departs. At the beginning of the Pentecostal

Administration, the twelve are mightily endued and are able to brave the opposition of their religious rulers. At the end they have been forced from the holy city and their cause is lost. Only a lone apostle, a prisoner in Rome, remains as God's ambassador. All the power he has lies in his weakness.

While Peter and the other apostles to the Jews continue to preach the evangel of the kingdom with some initial success, Christ appears as a blinding light on a road to the nations, and calls the blasphemer and outrager, Paul, as an apostle, or special messenger, to the nations. Over time, the Spirit of Christ commits to Paul an evangel different from "the evangel of the kingdom." While Christ is the light of the world, He specifically chooses Paul "for a light of the nations . . . to be for salvation as far as the limits of the earth" (Acts 13:47). Christ commits to Paul "the evangel of the grace of God" (Acts 20:24), but so long as the door to the millennial earthly kingdom remains open for the Jews, he preaches the evangel of the kingdom to them.

The Administration of the Grace of God

As Israel's second rejection of their King begins to shut the door to His coming earthly kingdom, Paul opens a door of faith to the nations, preaching justification by faith.

Having had a "spirit of stupor" (Romans 11:8) put upon them by God, the leaders of Israel finally reject the good news of the coming earthly kingdom ruled by Christ. At the close of the Book of Acts, Paul describes this stupor by citing, as Christ did in Matthew 13:14-15, Isaiah 6:9-10. This marvelous prophecy has had a threefold fulfillment in Israel: when they rejected Jehovah (Isaiah 6:9-10), when they rejected the Lord (Matthew 13:14-15), and when, in this case, they rejected the testimony of the Spirit through His apostles (Acts 28:25-27):

> **Go to the people and say,**
> **"In hearing, you will be hearing, and may by no means be understanding,**
> **And observing, you will be observing, and may by no means be perceiving,"**
> **For stoutened is the heart of this people,**
> **And with their ears heavily they hear,**
> **And with their eyes they squint,**
> **Lest at some time they may be perceiving with their eyes,**

And with their ears should be hearing,
And with their heart may be understanding,
And should be turning about,
And I shall be healing them.

Paul then writes, "Let it be known to you, then, that to the nations was dispatched this salvation of God, and they will hear" (Acts 28:28).

Thus, the kingdom proclamation ceased and the history of the kingdom ends—not to be resumed until the present administration of God's grace, in which the evangel goes direct to the nations apart from Israel's mediacy, is finished.

Peter, James, John, and Jude write letters specifically to the believing Jews for guidance as the kingdom expectation wanes. An unknown author writes the Book of Hebrews specifically for them. As Mr. Knoch has written in the Concordant Commentary:

Hebrews resumes the subject of the book of Acts. Paul's epistles are a parenthesis in God's administrations. In Acts the kingdom is proclaimed, and rejected by the nation of Israel as a whole. Yet there was a remnant who believed. Of these the Hellenists followed the revelations given to Paul and found a new and a celestial destiny. But the Hebrews, associated with the twelve apostles and James, whose destiny is the kingdom as promised by the prophets, are left in a distressing situation due to the national defection of Israel. What is to become of them during the time that the nation stumbles? The kingdom cannot come until after the fullness of the nations has come in. That could hardly be during their lifetime. The book of Hebrews deals with the problem of these Pentecostal believers and takes them back to the same position as was occupied by the patriarchs and prophets of old, as explained in the eleventh chapter. They died in faith, not having received the promises . . .

As the faith of the Pentecostal believers rested on signs and wonders and miracles in anticipation of the powers of the kingdom, some fell away when these manifestations ceased and the promised kingdom failed to appear. Their apostasy is dealt with in the sixth and tenth chapters—passages which can have no application in the present administration of grace, but which have hung as a cloud over the heads of those who imagine themselves in a similar position. Saints in Israel were conditionally pardoned. Its continuance depended upon their extension of this pardon to the other nations, as in the parable of the ten thousand talent debtor. The pardon could be and was withdrawn. It is not in force now. We have the infinitely higher favor of justification [through the epistles of Paul, the apostle to the nations].

Now that the kingdom evangel has been finally rejected, Paul is able to reveal to "the ecclesia which is [Christ's] body" the transcendent truths applicable for today in his prison or "perfection" epistles—Ephesians, Philippians, and Colossians.

Paul discloses the celestial destiny of the ecclesia and the secret of the evangel of the grace of God. With the Pentecostal administration completed, Paul inaugurates "the administration of the grace of God . . . [which is also] the administration of the secret, which has been concealed from the eons in God" (Ephesians 3:2, 9). Paul divulges that God shall reconcile all estranged beings—whether on the earth or in the heavens—to Himself through Christ Who makes this peace possible through the blood of His cross; and that He shall use the ecclesia to make known to the sovereignties and authorities among the celestials the multifarious wisdom of God (Colossians 1:20, Ephesians 3:10).

Paul provides for the transmission of the evangel of the grace of God by instructing Timothy (and undoubtedly many others) to pass on what he has learned to faithful men who shall be competent to teach others also (II Timothy 2:2).

Paul explains that the dispensational period known as the administration of the grace of God will be followed by a time of wrath, and that those under his teaching are delivered from that day (I Thessalonians 5:2, II Thessalonians 2:2, Romans 5:9). Before the day of Yahweh comes, they will be assembled together to the Lord at His presence (II Thessalonians 2:1).

As Satan, transfigured into a messenger of light, works through his ministers of righteousness (II Corinthians 11:14,15), the apostasy, or falling away from the truth, proceeds apace. Men develop the creeds of Christendom through philosophy; the beliefs and traditions of men take hold, and many in the ecclesia are despoiled—robbed of the transcendent truth of God's grace. Theologians, through the wisdom of men, mix together the evangel of the kingdom and the evangel of the grace of God into one contradictory doctrine. Men change the basis of salvation from simple faith in Christ—the Son and Image of the Invisible God—to belief in a mysterious and incomprehensible trinity of co-equal, co-eternal "persons." Men introduce Hel, the Norse goddess of the underworld, into translations of the Scriptures. The salvation of some and the eternal torment of many replaces the truth of the reconciliation of all, obscuring God's "purpose of the eons" and casting aspersions upon His boundless love and power to save.

This brings us to the present, the time preceding the instantaneous transformation and snatching away to celestial realms of the body of Christ, and the subsequent Day of God's Indignation on earth.

Chapter XIV

THE SNATCHING AWAY OF THE ECCLESIA

There is no hint in the Hebrew Scriptures that individuals within the nations would one day have access to God apart from the mediacy of Israel. Only in Paul's epistles do we learn of "the glorious riches of this secret among the nations" (Colossians 1:27). Likewise, only in the writings of Paul do we learn that Christ is coming in the air to snatch away with Him "the ecclesia which is His body" into celestial realms prior to His coming to the earth to rule from Jerusalem as its triumphant Monarch. In those writings, this "snatching away," commonly called the "rapture," is described and explained.

The Transformation Into Celestials

How is it that we shall be able to ascend to the air, and accompany Him to the celestial spheres? II Corinthians 5:17 explains: "So that, if anyone is in Christ, there is a new creation: the primitive passed by. Lo! there has come new!" As our earthly bodies are not fit for inhabiting the heavenly realms, a change must take place, and it indeed shall: "And according as we wear the image of the soilish, we should be wearing the image also of the celestial" (I Corinthians 15:49).

Paul explains how it will happen:

Now we do not want you to be ignorant, brethren, concerning those who are reposing, lest you may sorrow according as the rest, also, who have no expectation. For, if we are believing that Jesus died and rose, thus also, those who are put to repose, will God, through Jesus, lead forth together

with Him. For this we are saying to you by the word of the Lord, that we, the living, who are surviving to the presence of the Lord, should by no means outstrip those who are put to repose, for the Lord Himself will be descending from heaven with a shout of command, with the voice of the Chief Messenger, and with the trumpet of God, and the dead in Christ shall be rising first. Thereupon we, the living who are surviving, shall at the same time be snatched away together with them in clouds, to meet the Lord in the air. And thus shall we always be together with the Lord. So that, console one another with these words (I Thessalonians 4:13-18).

Paul mentions it again in I Corinthians 15:20-23:

Yet now Christ has been roused from among the dead, the Firstfruit of those who are reposing. For since, in fact, through a man came death, through a Man, also, come the resurrection of the dead. For even as, in Adam, all are dying, thus also, in Christ, shall all be vivified. Yet each in his own class: the Firstfruit, Christ; thereupon those who are Christ's in His presence . . . (I Corinthians 15:20-23).

Notice the precision of the language here. All are not dead in Adam, but "are dying." True, most are dead in Adam, but a large number of believers will be alive (though dying) who will be "snatched away to meet the Lord in the air." And Paul explains how quickly it will happen:

Lo! a secret to you am I telling! We all, indeed, shall not be put to repose, yet we all shall be changed, in an instant, in the twinkle of an eye, at the last trump. For He will be trumpeting, and the dead will be roused incorruptible, and we shall be changed. For this corruption must put on incorruption, and this mortal put on immortality (I Corinthians 15:51-53).

What Our Celestial Bodies Will Be Like

For our realm is inherent in the heavens, out of which we are awaiting a Saviour also, the Lord, Jesus Christ, Who will transfigure the body of our humiliation, to conform it to the body of His glory, in accord with the operation which enables Him even to subject all to Himself (Philippians 3:20, 21).

Our bodies will be like His in glory. On the mount of transformation, Peter and James and John glimpsed Christ's celestial body: ". . . and [Christ] was transformed in front of them. And His face shines as the sun, yet His garments became white as the light" (Matthew 17:2). Paul had a similar experience on the road to Damascus: "Suddenly a light out of heaven flashes about him" (Acts 9:3). Light will emanate from our celestial bodies, and I believe we can safely surmise that they will be made of light. Already, figuratively, we are "light in the Lord" and "children of light" (Ephesians 5:8, 9). And we shall be made "competent for a part of the allotment of the saints, in light" (Colossians 1:12).

Our celestial bodies that will house our spirits are already prepared for us:

> **For we are aware that, if our terrestrial tabernacle house should be demolished, we have a building in God, a house not made by hands, eonian, in the heavens. For in this also we are groaning, longing to be dressed in our habitation which is out of heaven, if so be that, being dressed also, we shall not be found naked. For we also, who are in the tabernacle, are groaning, being burdened, on which we are not wanting to be stripped but to be dressed, that the mortal may be swallowed up by life. Now He Who produces us for this same longing is God, Who is also giving us the earnest of the spirit (II Corinthians 5:1-5).**

Our spirits await the Lord out of heaven, and our spirits "are groaning" in anticipation. But do we wait and groan alone?

> **For the premonition of the creation is awaiting the unveiling of the sons of God. For to vanity was the creation subjected, not voluntarily, but because of Him Who subjects it, in expectation that the creation itself, also, shall be freed from the slavery of corruption into the glorious freedom of the children of God. For we are aware that the entire creation is groaning and travailing together until now. Yet not only so, but we ourselves also, who have the firstfruit of the spirit, we ourselves also, are groaning in ourselves, awaiting the sonship, the deliverance of our body (Romans 8:19-23).**

We and the entire creation are groaning. All of creation is out of God, and He is Spirit, Light and Love. All creation has come through Christ, and "all has its cohesion in Him" (Colossians 1:17). At the core of all is Love, Light, and Spirit. Within everything—within every atom—there is a kind of unconscious predisposition for it to become what it was purposed ultimately to be. The entire creation "knows" what is destined to be, and that is why it is groaning.

How Do We Wait For This Glorious Event?

If, then, you were roused together with Christ, be seeking that which is above, where Christ is, sitting at the right hand of God. Be disposed to that which is above, not to that on the earth, for you died, and your life is hid together with Christ in God. Whenever Christ, our Life, should be manifested, then you also shall be manifested together with Him in glory (Colossians 3:1-4).

Who Gets Snatched Away?

Who will go? Who will be snatched away to meet the Lord in the air when he descends and calls His own to Him there? In these degenerate days, Christendom is composed of many who are not even believers. To some, the Scriptures cannot be "modernized" fast enough to suit their lifestyles and philosophies. They have not heard His call in life, so certainly will not respond to it in death. We may be sure they will not go.

But there are many who have been called, who rely on Him for salvation, but who live in a fog of tradition and deception, and know little of the Scriptures, and less of the truth for the present, who have hardly heard of the "secrets," and cling to the teaching of our Lord and His twelve apostles concerning the kingdom, rather than the message of Paul for the nations.

Other believers claim to have exclusive knowledge and a special position. Some are sure they belong to the 144,000 on *earth*. For a time, I belonged to a Pentecostal denomination which taught that all who were to be saved had to be baptized according to their specific formula, and had to live a righteous life afterwards according to a set of denominational rules. It is useless to catalogue all the conflicting claims, for all but one must be wrong, and who knows if even that is altogether correct?

Faith in Christ is sufficient, no matter how faulty one's other beliefs. The members of the ecclesia which is the body of Christ are under grace even if they do not acknowledge it or understand it. False belief is a "missing the mark;" that is, sin, but for us with faith in the Son of God, "where sin increases, grace superexceeds" (Romans 5:20).

Even the personal "beliefs" of each saint change from time to time. How greatly mine have! When we first *really* believed, for salvation through the blood of Christ, we may have thought that it was due to our *repentance*, and our sins were *pardoned*, and we had *entered the kingdom.* But these things are not for the joint body, for the saints in it are *justified* and *reconciled,* and, *when they believe,* are sealed with the holy spirit of *promise,* which is an earnest of the enjoyment of our allotment, to the deliverance of that which has been procured, that is, we are pre-expectants in the Christ (Ephesians 1:12-14), and will hear Him when He calls from the air. The spirit that we receive when we believe determines our place and portion, of which it is a part, not our ignorance or mistaken beliefs.

Almost all who have attained to maturity in Christ have had to put aside some childish and flawed beliefs. Being part of the snatching away of the saints is a question of God's designating us beforehand in love for sonship, not of our understanding, or appreciation, or response. It is in accord with His own purpose, and the grace which He has given to us in Christ Jesus before times eonian (II Timothy 1:9).

Paul prays for those who are sealed with the holy spirit of promise, for a further spirit of wisdom to perceive what is the expectation of their calling and the riches of their allotment and the power present at the rousing of Christ (Ephesians 1:14). This makes it evident that they lacked this added endowment, and that the earnest of the spirit, which is the portion of all, does not include a knowledge of the higher truths for today. Yet this does not invalidate our pre-expectancy. Under the law, and even in the evangel of the kingdom, some response is necessary, or the blessing is withdrawn. Not so in grace. It operates even better in the midst of failure and opposition than otherwise, for these provide a background for its display.

It is a common fallacy to reason that our destiny is in some way dependent on ourselves. In the higher circles of Europe they have a sarcastic saying, "A man cannot be too careful in the choice of his ancestors." We all came into the world without being asked the time, the place, or the circumstances. Either it was a favorable or fiendish fate, or the work of a selecting, supervising Subjector. We who love and worship Him can have no doubt on this score, for He has revealed to us that He chose us in Christ before the disruption (Ephesians 1:4). A child is not disinherited because it is weak or immature. None of us is fit for the glory about to be revealed in us. The very thought of such selfishness dims and darkens the grace of God, the display of which, throughout the universe, is the chief excuse for our existence.

Must We Watch?

Must we be alert and watching when He comes for us? No. This idea comes from those who misapply to themselves scriptures that concern the return of Christ to Israel at the beginning of the Millennium. Our Lord warned the living saints of Israel to be watching, for only those who watch will be taken along when He comes to Israel. To them the Son of Mankind comes as a thief, and some will be received and others left for judgment, as it was in the days of Noah (Matthew 24:37-51). The highest in the kingdom are those who earned it by their attainments and sufferings. Only those who were true to their Lord throughout his ministry and rejection will occupy positions in the coming earthly kingdom. Paul will have no place there at all. He, as we, already will have been roused to glory before the resurrection of the just takes place in the earthly kingdom. He expected nothing less:

The Lord will be rescuing me from every wicked work and will be saving me for His *celestial* **kingdom: to Whom be glory for the eons of the eons. Amen! (II Timothy 4:18).**

We who are part of the body of Christ are exhorted to watch, but in a very different way. As the next chapter shows, the seven years following the snatching away will be the worst era in earth's history. Darkness will cover the earth, and murkiness the peoples (Isaiah 60:2). It is true that the world today is also in darkness, but not so his saints: "Now you, brethren, are not in darkness, that the day may be overtaking you, as a thief" (I Thessalonians 5:2):

For you are all sons of the light and sons of the day. We are not of the night nor of the darkness. Consequently then, we should not be drowsing, even as the rest, but we may be watching, and sober. For those who are drowsing are drowsing at night, and those who are drunk are drunk at night. Yet we, being of the day, may be sober, putting on the cuirass of faith and love, and the helmet, the expectation of salvation, for God did not appoint us to indignation, but to the procuring of salvation through our Lord Jesus Christ, Who died for our sakes, that, *whether we may be watching or drowsing,* **we should be living** *at the same time together* **with Him. Wherefore, console one another, and edify one another, according as you are doing also (I Thessalonians 5:4-11).**

Regrettably, most of today's saints are drunk or drowsing. Even those who have never tasted a drop of alcohol are intoxicated with the spirits of delusion and error. And we who claim to be sober, and not sleeping, are we not drowsy? God pity us if we were dealt with in the same way as those who watch for the kingdom! If we received our desserts we would be with those who lament and gnash their teeth.

Consolation and edification are ours only because God deals with us differently. There is no penalty if we fail to keep awake and sober. There are doubtless some saints, such as Paul, Timothy, and Titus, who obeyed these exhortations, but what about us and the rest? We certainly don't deserve to be vivified and snatched away to meet the Lord in the air, if it depends upon our watchfulness and sobriety!

Here we see, as perhaps nowhere else, the practical operation of the transcendent grace which is our portion in this administration. At its close none will be penalized for their past by being rejected at the snatching away, as in the case of the resurrection of the saints of Israel. In order to stress this, the Scriptures repeat the thought by using two words, to emphasize the fact that all will be snatched away *at the same time together* (I Thessalonians 4:17).

Why We Are Snatched Away

If our being called, justified, snatched away, and glorified is completely a matter of grace, the reason for it must transcend us greatly. And it does:

Yet God, being rich in mercy, because of His vast love with which He loves us (we also being dead to the offenses and the lusts), vivifies us together in Christ (in grace are you saved!) and rouses us together and seats us together among the celestials, in Christ Jesus, that, in the oncoming eons, He should be *displaying the transcendent riches of His grace* in His kindness to us in Christ Jesus (Ephesians 2:4-7).

Through the transformation of unworthy, dying mortals into immortal beings of light who operate with their Saviour above all sovereignty and authority, Christ will indeed be "displaying the transcendent riches of His grace" to His celestial creations. We have seen that it is God the Father's purpose to become All in all of His creations. This He accomplishes, over the course of the eons, by subjecting the universe to Christ, the Son of His Love. Christ is God's Image, His

Complement, or That Which makes God completely known to His creation. Christ will reconcile all heavenly and earthly beings to God the Father through the blood of His cross (Colossians 1:18-20). The ecclesia, in turn, is spoken of as Christ's complement, the medium through which the All in all is being completed (Ephesians 1:22-23).

As part of Christ's glorified body, the saints become beings of the highest order. Paul writes that the saints shall judge, or set right, the world as well as messengers (I Corinthians 6:2, 3). This does not mean that the saints will condemn the world, but rather rule it during the oncoming eons. While the saints in Israel will rule Christ's kingdom on earth, the saints who are members of Christ's body will administer the rest of the universe, directing and controlling the messengers to the utmost bounds of creation. By the power of Christ, His glorified ecclesia will subdue all celestial rebellion and enmity, playing its ordained part in "completing the All in all." No longer acting as fallible humans, the members of Christ's Body will operate as an inseparable part of the Infallible Light of the world.

The great work of the reconciliation of the universe—the heavens in all their magnitude, the celestial regions with all their multitude of inhabitants—is to be carried out by Christ, operating in and through that glorified ecclesia which is His body, His complement.

We are foreknown, predesignated, called, justified, snatched away, and glorified, not for any blessings that may accrue to us, although we shall be blessed beyond all measure in the process, but that the supreme glory of His grace might be lauded throughout the whole universe. Paul writes in Ephesians 1:11 that we are those "being designated beforehand according to the purpose of the One Who is operating all in accord with the counsel of His will, that we should be for the laud of His glory."

The Celestial Realm—A Busy Place

As we can see, contrary to popular theology, heaven is not solely a place of rest and bliss. The bliss that will be ours in our future state will come more from our being conformed to the glorious body of our Lord, and ever with Him, than from our being in any special locality. For us, the heavenly realms will be a scene of intense activity. Satan will still be there when we are snatched away. It is not until midway through the period of indignation that Michael battles with Satan and casts him from the heavenly realms to the earth:

And a battle occurred in heaven. Michael and his messengers battle with the dragon, and the dragon battles, and its messengers. And they are not strong enough for him, neither was their place still found in heaven.

And the great dragon was cast out, the ancient serpent called Adversary and Satan, who is deceiving the whole inhabited earth. It was cast to the earth, and its messengers were cast with it (Revelation 12:7-9).

We shall witness that event from the celestial standpoint, and begin to comprehend how the Supreme Spirit operates all.

Many of the saints have wished to be there when Christ comes in great glory to the Mount of Olives, to set up His kingdom. Some have never even heard of our pre-expectant meeting with Him in the air. Will they be disappointed? Will we miss that marvelous sight, when every eye shall see Him, even the nation who stabbed Him? Absolutely not!

To us, seven years prior to His return to the Mount of Olives, He descends alone, unattended by any angelic host, for He Himself is the Chief Messenger, and He Himself will blow the trumpet of God, which will wake the dead.

But to Israel He comes attended by a heavenly host. We read that, "coming is the Lord my God, And all the saints are with Him" (Zechariah 14:5). All the highest and holiest of the host of heaven will be with Him on Mount Olivet, and we shall always be together with the Lord (I Thessalonians 4:17). Even though our allotment and mission are among the celestials, He would not have us absent from the moment of His highest terrestrial triumph.

Before He comes for us, we are ambassadors on this earth for Him (II Corinthians 5:20). As He snatches away His ecclesia, His ambassadors are withdrawn. The administration of the grace of God ends. Man's day reaches its climax, and because of it comes God's Day of Indignation against unfaithful Israel and the unbelieving nations.

Chapter XV

THE DAY OF INDIGNATION

Now let no one be seducing you with empty words, for because of these things God's indignation is coming on the sons of stubbornness (Ephesians 5:6).

"Whenever, then, you may be perceiving the abomination of desolation, which is declared through Daniel the prophet, standing in the holy place (let him who is reading apprehend!); then let those in Judea flee into the mountains. Let him who is on the housetop not descend to take away the things out of his house. And let him who is in the field not turn back behind him to pick up his cloak."

"Now woe to those who are pregnant and those suckling in those days! Now be praying that your flight may not be occurring in winter, nor yet on a Sabbath, for then shall be great affliction, such as has not occurred from the beginning of the world till now: neither under any circumstances may be occurring. And, except those days were discounted, no flesh at all would be saved. Yet because of the chosen, those days shall be discounted" (Matthew 24:15-22).

The Desolator

Now comes the culmination of "man's day." The human religion and government desired by Cush, Nimrod and their followers back in Babylon, at the very beginning of this present wicked eon, comes into full and foredoomed being on this earth. We know from the book of Daniel that this horrendous time lasts seven years. The whole era is marked by man's ultimate attempt to attain perfection apart from God. The Wild Beast and the False Prophet, animated by the power of the Dragon (Satan), set up the world empire and the world federation of religion.

In the midst of these seven years, comes "the abomination of desolation," the presence in the holy place (presumably the rebuilt temple in Jerusalem) of the Wild Beast invigorated by the spirit of Satan.

The Adversary of the True God and His Christ, a created being, obtains worship as creator; the words of the father of lies are welcomed as truth; and the ruiner and slanderer is accepted as the saviour of mankind.

It might be well for us to consider what the Scriptures reveal concerning this personage who commits "the abomination of desolation," this Desolator. We find him designated in the Hebrew Scriptures as:

The Assyrian (Isaiah 10:5-6, 30:27-33),
King of Babylon (Isaiah 14:4),
Son of the Dawn (Isaiah 14:12),
The Little Horn (Daniel 7:8, 9-12),
The King of Strong Presence (Daniel 8:23),
The Coming Governor (Daniel 9:26) and
The Willful, Self-Exalting King (Daniel 11:36).

In the Greek Scriptures he is designated as:

The Man of Lawlessness (II Thessalonians 2:3),
The Son of Destruction (II Thessalonians 2:3, 4),
The Lawless One (II Thessalonians 2:8) and
The Wild Beast (Revelation 13:1, 2).

Our Lord made prophetic allusion to him when speaking to the sons of Israel concerning His own ministry among them, saying, "I have come in the name of My Father, and you are not getting Me. If another should come in his own name, him you will get" (John 5:43). Mankind as a whole, during this entire eon, rejects the True God and accepts the imitation.

He will be the "Superman," posing as the great humanitarian, the friend of men, and the special friend of the Jewish people, many of whom will be persuaded by him that he has come to usher in the golden age as pictured by their prophets, who will hail him as their Messiah. He will intoxicate men with the strong delusion of his never-varying success. When he receives the death blow of the sword and is resurrected (Revelation 13:3), he will have lost none of these powers, but will be, in addition, the embodiment of all kinds of wickedness and blasphemy.

A puny man, without energizing aid from another source, could never attain such power and influence. And neither are we left to conjecture as to where he gets it. Paul says his presence is in accord with the operation of Satan with all power and signs and false miracles (II

Thessalonians 2:9), while John tells us that the dragon gives it (the Wild Beast) its power and its throne and great authority (Revelation 13:2).

In the disguise of the "white horse rider" of the sixth chapter of Revelation, the Desolator will come, promising peace and prosperity. Many false messiahs have come and will come, but this is the greatest of all, the one "deceiving the whole inhabited earth" (Revelation 12:9). That he will empower a covenant with Israel under which their ancient form of sacrificial worship will be restored, is but one indication of his great power to delude.

Not only will the Israelites receive him, but the gentile nations—the sons of stubbornness—will hail him as their leader, king, and saviour, for he will be the last head exercising world dominion, to whom "authority will be given over every tribe and people and language and nation" (Revelation 13:7). When, in the middle of the seven-year period, he seats himself "in the temple of God, demonstrating that he himself is God" (II Thessalonians 2:4), his sinister associate, the False Prophet, will demand that all worship the image of the Wild Beast, and the Dragon. Those who refuse will be killed!

Then will be realized the confederation of nations headed up by the Man of Lawlessness, the king who does what is acceptable to himself, exalting himself and magnifying himself over every deity, and to whom is given authority to do as he wills forty-two months, or three and a half years (Revelation 13:5, Daniel 7:25). The unbelieving Jews along with all the rest of mankind join this great alliance to blot out the worship of the True God from the face of the earth.

The Mark of the Wild Beast

The "mark" of the Wild Beast will be the emblem or flag or symbol of the world confederation. It must be worn, or be branded, in a most conspicuous place so that any one may be able to tell at a glance if any one is not a worshiper of the Beast. Such a mark or badge has often been used to indicate political or religious affiliations, and usually consists of some appropriate and significant design expressive of the character or purpose of the unity which it represents. As all who belong to the body of Christ will be in celestial realms with the Lord by this time, all the world will gladly receive this badge as the pledge of their allegiance to the world federation of religion and government, except the few Jews who will be faithful to Jehovah.

666

All will be obliged to have one of three marks to indicate their worship of the Wild Beast: either its symbol, its name, or its number. The number, we are told, is the number of humanity. This has nothing to do with its name. The number seven, which is used throughout the Book of Revelation, is significant of sufficiency and completion. This is its meaning in Hebrew. The number six comes one short of this. It is significant of insufficiency and incompletion. This entire era is marked by man's supreme attempt to attain perfection apart from God. All his achievements fall well short of the divine standard. He accomplishes the federation of mankind—except for a few Jews. He unites all the world under one religion—except for a handful in Judea. He conquers all who oppose—except Christ. In everything humanity falls one step short of its goal. Hence its number is 666. This is the summit of all man's efforts.

With the return of the Lord to earth, man's day comes to its predestined end. The wisdom of men is proven to be what it is—stupidity with God (I Corinthians 3:19).

We, as humans, seem almost incapable of grasping the realities of the awful horrors of the event closing this "present wicked eon." The Dragon, the Wild Beast, the False Prophet, and the kings of the whole inhabited earth with their armies gather in the heart of Palestine, between the mountains of Israel, to do battle with the White Horse Rider and His armies from heaven, Who is Lord of lords and King of kings. Imagine the sun darkened, the moon not giving her beams, and the blackness of the sky stabbed by millions of menacing meteors, thick as a barrage of bullets in battle, when the stars fall!

At the same time an earthquake sways the earth to and fro—an earthquake such as has never occurred since mankind came to be on the earth, so that the mountains and islands leave their places! Imagine the great cities of the nations with all their wonderful skyscrapers falling! Think of the calamity of hail, each stone as large as a talent weight (85 to 114 pounds) falling from heaven on men! Can we imagine a more desperate situation? Is it any wonder that the kings of the earth and the magnates and the captains and the rich, the strong, the slaves, and freemen go scurrying to the caves and cry for the rocks of the mountains to fall on them?

Christ's Triumphant Return to Earth

Yet all these things are but a prelude to the most momentous vision earth will ever see! All of a sudden, the black pall wrapping the earth in midnight darkness will roll back and reveal the sign of the Son of Mankind in all His glory. Like a new luminary, blotting out the sun in its brightness, there appears the most glorious majesty of the epiphany of the coming of Christ—the True White Horse Rider from heaven. Just as the lightning flashes forth from the sullen clouds, so will be the presence of the Son of Mankind. The veil of pitch darkness will roll back like a scroll and the glorious One will be revealed from heaven in all His power and majesty.

Christ returns in glory to the Mount of Olives and destroys the armies arrayed against Israel with "the blade which is coming out of [His] mouth" (Revelation 19:21). One mighty blow from above renders the Wild Beast and the False Prophet powerless. They are captured and cast alive ("living") for eonion torment into "the lake of fire burning with sulphur" (Revelation 19:20). The kings of the earth and their armies of the sons of stubbornness are destroyed. Birds of the air and beasts of the field feast upon their bodies. The Stone of Daniel 2:35 will have fallen, and with one blow the dominion and misrule of the Gentiles is ended, and "The world kingdom [becomes] our Lord's and His Christ's and He shall be reigning for the eons of the eons" (Revelation 11:15).

Then, when Satan, the chief of the authority of the air (Ephesians 2:2), the suzerain of the world mights of darkness and spiritual forces of wickedness among the celestials (Ephesians 6:11,12) is bound and cast into the abyss, locked and sealed so he cannot deceive the nations until the thousand years may be finished (Revelation 20:3), then will begin the earth's jubilee, when

. . . the kingdom and the authority and the majesty of the kingdom under all the heavens is granted to the people of the supremacies. The kingdom is an eonian kingdom, and all authorities shall serve and hearken to it (Daniel 7:27).

Let's step into this millennial kingdom.

Chapter XVI

The Millennial Eon

I come to perceive in the visions of the night, and behold! with the clouds of the heavens, He arrives as the son of a mortal ... And to Him is granted authority, and esteem, and a kingdom, and all the peoples, the races, the languages are serving Him. His authority is an eonian authority which passes not away, and His kingdom that is not pawned (Daniel 7:13, 14).

And in that era your people shall be delivered, everyone found written in the scroll (Daniel 12:1).

The sovereignty of the earth becomes our Lord's and His Messiah's for the final two eons known as "the eons of the eons" (Revelation 11:15).

Christ returns to the Mount of Olives. The hour of judging the earth is over. Christ is King. He reigns. A new eonian evangel comes into being based on the fear of God as the Creator of all. Jesus resurrects the saints in Israel, and they commence their righteous reign over the earth. "Happy and holy is he who is having part in the former resurrection: over these the second death has no jurisdiction, but they will be priests of God and of Christ, and they will be reigning with Him the thousand years" (Revelation 20:6).

Hundreds of prophesies from the Hebrew and Greek Scriptures are fulfilled. This prayer is answered: "Thy kingdom come. Thy will be done, as in heaven, on earth also" (Matthew 6:10). The meek inherit the earth. God gives His people a new spirit. He writes His law on their hearts. The kingdom is thus within them.

The question of Isaiah 66:8, "Should a nation be born at one time?" is answered. In their utmost extremity Messiah has come and redeemed His people, restoring the kingdom, and making Israel the head of all the nations. Jerusalem arises from her ashes, and becomes the glory of the whole earth. The scene is one of great happiness. People are going about their business undisturbed. There is an air of prosperity and calm. No wars take place, no massive acts of violence. No one seems to be afraid. There is much traffic between the leading cities of the world and Jerusalem, which has become the world capital, and all nations send their representatives there. The law goes forth from Zion, and the word of the Lord from Jerusalem.

Yes, following His own unveiling, Christ has set up His kingdom, and He is ruling from His capital city. Israel has taken up the kingly and priestly roles allotted to her at Sinai, and officiates with Christ in this dual capacity. For Christ is a kingly Priest. This Priest does not accept sacrifices for sin, for sin has been dealt with once and to a finality at Golgotha. But He accepts offerings from the people and He blesses the people accordingly with kingly blessings.

The Reign of Righteousness

Though Messiah will be reigning as the Prince of Peace in that day, it will be a reign based on righteousness and law. The least infraction of the kingdom code, as expounded in the Sermon on the Mount, will receive immediate judgment. The entire catalogue of sins will be adjudicated according to the inflexible law of righteousness that characterizes that reign of the kingdom, when judgment will be immediate and summary.

We have a graphic picture of the severe order of adjudication in that day in Ananias and Sapphira, in the Pentecostal Administration, when the kingdom was being preached with the authority of heaven attending. Immediately, without recourse to mercy, when they lied to the Holy Spirit, they were each struck dead right in front of Peter! And it is written of the kingdom administration:

> **One doing deceit shall not dwell within My house;**
> **One speaking falsehoods shall not be established**
>   **in front of My eyes.**

> In the mornings I shall efface all the wicked of the land,
> To cut off from the city of Yahweh
>   all contrivers of lawlessness (Psalms 101:7, 8).

In the future day of the kingdom, Gehenna, the ravine just below Jerusalem where the offal was burned, will again be the incinerator of the city and the receptacle of the bodies of criminals and transgressors of the law. It will be a place of public display, as an object lesson against lawlessness in that day. Isaiah verifies this by giving us a vision of the severity with which judgment shall be meted out to transgressors:

> "And it comes, according to the monthly quota in its month,
> And according to the sabbath's quota in its sabbath,
> All flesh shall come to worship
> Before Me in Jerusalem," says Yahweh.
> "And they fare forth and see the corpses of the mortals,
> The transgressors against Me,
> For their worm shall not die,
> And their fire shall not be quenched,
> And they become a repulsion to all flesh" (Isaiah 66:23, 24).

Here we find that all who come to Jerusalem from month to month and sabbath to sabbath to worship, shall go forth and look upon the corpses of men who have transgressed God's law, and there in Gehenna fire, that is kept continually burning day and night, the portions of the bodies not burned will be infested by repulsive maggots!

Israel Judged by the Twelve Apostles

The government of the nation of Israel in the future inhabited earth will be in the hands of the apostles, which explains in part why there must be just twelve, one for each tribe. Concerning this, the Lord Jesus made prophetic promise to them in the closing days of His earthly ministry, saying:

> **Verily, I am saying to you that you, who follow Me, in the renascence, whenever the Son of Mankind should be sitting on His glorious throne, you, also, shall be seated on twelve thrones, judging the twelve tribes of Israel (Matthew 19:28).**

Just as twelve is the number of government and the kingdom, and twelve apostles are chosen to rule the twelve tribes of Israel, there are also twelve times twelve thousand (144,000) sealed out of every tribe of the sons of Israel (Revelation 7:4) for kingdom administrators, who will have jurisdiction over the nations of the earth in that day, shepherding them with an iron club (Revelation 12:5).

Yahweh's Sanctuary

The millennial sanctuary will not be built in the new city of Jerusalem, but about eighteen miles north of it, near Shiloh, where the tabernacle rested after the sons of Israel conquered the land, and where it remained until the death of Eli. A study of the closing chapters of Ezekiel gives a wonderful vision of divine wisdom in the outlay of everything for that glorious era. Nothing will be crowded, but all will be located according to specifications in keeping with the august administration of that eon. The new sanctuary will occupy a space of 500 reeds on each side (Ezekiel 42:15-20), which is equivalent to a little more than a square mile. According to calculations made from information in chapter eight of Daniel, the sanctuary will be dedicated two years, eight months and five days after the millennial reign begins. This glorious edifice will have the admiration of all the world for its hallowed location and architectural beauty.

And then to link Jerusalem with the sanctuary, this passage of Isaiah will be fulfilled:

And there comes to be a highway and a clean one.
And the holy way shall it be called.
The unclean shall not pass there,
And it shall be for those going that way (Isaiah 35:8).

This highway will be a magnificent elevated boulevard, about eighteen miles long, reaching from the city to the sanctuary called "the holy way," on which the ransomed of God shall walk, with eonian joy upon their heads.

The Better Covenant

Few phrases are more confusing and misleading than "the New Testament." The majority of Christians have had planted in their minds the erroneous idea which causes them to think of the Greek Scriptures as "the New Testament" and the Hebrew Scriptures as "the Old Testament." Yet, in truth, the "new covenant," or "testament," is found in the "Old Testament." It has never been in force yet, and the "New Testament" times will not come until after the coming indignation when Jehovah calls Israel and Judah back to Himself and the land of their fathers, and erects His sanctuary in the midst of them for the eon. Jeremiah gives it in full:

Behold, the days are coming, averring is Yahweh, when I will contract a new covenant with the house of Israel and the house of Judah. Not like the covenant which I contracted with their fathers in the day I held fast onto their hand to bring them forth from the country of Egypt, which covenant of Mine they themselves annulled while I was Possessor over them, avering is Yahweh. For this is the covenant which I shall contract with the house of Israel after those days, averring is Yahweh:
  I will put my law within them,
  And I shall write it on their heart;
  I will become their Elohim,
  And they shall become my people.
  No longer shall they teach, each man his associate,
  And each man his brother,
  Saying: Know Yahweh!
  For they all shall know Me,
  From the smallest of them to the greatest of them,
  Averring is Yahweh;
  For I shall pardon their depravity,
  And I shall no longer remember their sin (Jeremiah 31:31-34).

A discriminating study of this Scripture reveals that the "new covenant" is not for the nations, but for the "house of Israel and the house of Judah." It is confirmed to the "faithful" in Hebrews 8:8-12, which speaks of "the future inhabited earth" (Hebrews 1:6; 2:5), when they have been restored to their own land and received their Messiah. Then will He inscribe His law on their hearts and they shall walk in His statutes, and keep His judgments, and do them.

Festivals

Apparently only two festivals, or feasts, will be observed during the millennial reign—the Passover and Tabernacles, or Booths. They are very significant and worthy of our most earnest attention.

They will observe the Passover festival, but no Passover lamb will be slain, as Christ fulfilled that type in His sacrifice on the cross. It is then that the words of Christ will find the fulfillment which he spoke to His disciples when eating the last Passover with them:

And taking the cup and giving thanks, He gives it to them, saying, "Drink of it all, for this is My blood of the new covenant, that is shed for many for the pardon of sins. Now I am saying to you that under no circumstances may I be drinking henceforth of this, the product of the grapevine, till that day whenever I may be drinking it new with you in the kingdom of My Father" (Matthew 26:27-30).

Here in the kingdom, at the festival of the Passover, they will drink the cup of the new covenant, a memorial of the great deliverance which Christ's sacrifice on Golgotha accomplished. It will direct the minds and hearts of the people back to the cross.

The Festival of Booths will be observed by representatives of all nations, and will be a grand universal national thanksgiving for unfailing and fruitful seasons. Under the direction of King Messiah, once a year all nations will be under bond to send their representatives to Jerusalem to worship and return thanksgiving unto Jehovah for His abundant blessings upon them. (Zechariah 14:16-19).

The Missionary Enterprise

The missionary enterprise will be carried out by the ministers of God according to the program of the great commission decreed for that day. One reason for the sad failure experienced by our missionary movements today is that they are out of harmony with God's program. They are attempting to carry out Israel's future missionary work now, instead of giving heed to our own commission as ambassadors of Christ, to proclaim the evangel of the grace of God and the conciliation (II Corinthians 5:18-21).

During the Millennium, the sons of Israel will be called the "priests of Jehovah, and the ministers of our God" by the nations (Isaiah 61:6), and will go forth with the authority of reigning Messiah and fulfill the great commission as it is written:

"All authority in heaven and on earth was given to Me. Going then, *disciple all the nations*, baptizing them into the name of the Father and of the Son and of the holy spirit, teaching them to be keeping all, whatever I direct you. And lo! I am with you all the days till the conclusion of the eon! Amen!" (Matthew 28:18-20).

This Scripture, apportioned to its proper place in God's eonian administrations, exemplifies how ministers of the priestly nation of Israel shall go forth to all the world in the day of the Lord and *disciple all the nations*—not a few individuals out of the nations—teaching them to observe all whatever Messiah directs them. Then shall men of distant cities and strong nations come to Jerusalem to worship before Yahweh:

> Thus says Yahweh of hosts:
> "Still it shall be that many peoples shall come,
> And the dwellers of many cities.
> And the dwellers five cities shall go to another city saying,
> 'We are going assuredly to beseech the face of Yahweh,
> And to seek Yahweh of hosts;
>
> I am going, moreover.'
> And many peoples and staunch nations will come
> To seek Yahweh of hosts in Jerusalem,
> And to beseech the face of Yahweh."
> Thus says Yahweh of hosts:
> "In those days ten mortals from all the languages of the nations,
> will take fast hold.
> And they will take fast hold of the hem of a man, a Jew, saying
> 'We will go with you
> For we hear that the Lord is with you'" (Zechariah 8:20-23).

This gives us a glimpse of how eagerly the nations, in that day, will receive the glad message of the reigning Messiah in Jerusalem and come to worship before Him.

The Earth Relieved of Its Curse

When Adam sinned he dragged all creation down with him, and for six millennia the creation has been subjected to vanity and the slavery of corruption, groaning and travailing together. Yet in the future inhabited earth, under the beneficent reign of Messiah, creation itself, freed from the slavery of corruption will respond to His redemptive work. The desert will blossom as the rose, orchards will bend low with luscious fruit, vines will hang their purple clusters in the sun, the earth will again be a paradise and man its happy keeper (Isaiah 41:18-20). The renascence of the earth in the day of the Lord will display so unmistakably the omnipotence of Yahweh that all will acknowledge and ascribe to Him the glory and praise together with adoration and worship.

The Animal Kingdom Blessed

The animal kingdom, though innocent of the transgression of man, nevertheless has had to suffer all its consequences passively. But in the glorious era of the millennium, it will share the blessedness of the reign of the Prince of Peace:

> **Then the wolf will sojourn with the he-lamb,**
> **And the leopard will recline with the kid,**
> **And the calf and the sheltered lion will graze together,**
> **And a small lad will lead among them.**
> **And the young cow and the bear will graze together,**
> **And together they will recline their young.**
> **And the lion, as the beeve, will eat crushed straw.**
> **And the suckling will revel over the hole of the cobra,**
> **And on the light-shaft of a yellow viper the weanling his hand obtrudes.**
> **They will not do evil,**
> **Nor will they ruin in all My holy mountain,**
> **For full is the earth of the knowledge of Yahweh,**
> **As water for the sea floor is a covering (Isaiah 11:6-9).**

It is evident, from what is written, that everything in that blessed era will feel the boon of His glorious presence, save the serpent, the medium through which Satan beguiled Adam and Eve in Eden. Of it we are told:

> **"Then a wolf and a lambkin will graze alike,**
> **And the lion, as the beeve, will eat crushed straw,**
> **And the serpent has soil for its bread.**
> **They will not do evil,**
> **Nor ruin in all My holy mountain," says Yahweh (Isaiah 65:25).**

The whole creation, blighted by the curse of sin, shall be restored to its original beauty and harmony, save the serpent, which, though rendered harmless, apparently continues to grovel its way upon the ground, possibly as a sign of the ancient deception of Satan, and a warning of his future release for a little season at the close of the thousand years.

Yes, it will be a great change when Christ is King over all the earth, for then the profit will go to the toiler. However, it is well to remember that when Israel comes into its place as the royal priesthood of Yahweh, all nations, tribes, and peoples will be subject to their suzerainty, serving as herdsmen, farmers, and vineyardists (Isaiah 49:22, 23; 61:5, 6).

With the kingdom under all the heavens committed to the sovereignty of Israel (Daniel 7:27), then the promise to Abraham (Genesis 12:3) will be fulfilled, and "all the families of the earth will be blessed." Justice and security of life will be assured to all from the least to the greatest under this glorious reign of righteousness.

May He redress the humbled of the people,
May He save the sons of the needy,
And crush the exploiter (Psalms 72:4).

And the squares of the city shall be filled with
Boys and girls sporting in its squares (Zechariah 8:5).

What is the great King's ideal for child life revealed here? Play! But with what shall they play? With that from which we carefully and necessarily guard our little ones today. With no thought of harm, in that glorious era, the little dimple fist of a child may be entwined in the mane of a great shaggy lion and lead him about as a royal playmate!

The End of the Millennial Eon

The glorious era of the Millennium holds forth a prospect of the most favorable and perfect environment yet enjoyed by man, but it is so important to remember that it closes with the greatest apostasy of all the eons! Instead of the glory and honor and prosperity and well-being leading to heart allegiance to God, it results in an innumerable host, countless as the sands by the seashore, seizing the first opportunity that comes to show their latent hostility to Him and His saints.

This is described to us in Revelation 20:7-9:

And whenever the thousand years should be finished, Satan will be loosed out of his jail. And he will be coming out to deceive all the nations which are in the four corners of the earth, Gog and Magog, to be mobilizing them for battle, their number being as the sand of the sea. And they went up over the breadth of the earth, and surround the citadel of the saints and the beloved city. And fire descended from God out of heaven and devoured them.

How strange, in view of that Scripture, that so many believers should look upon the Millennium as the final eon, ushering in eternal happiness!

Christ is the King of Peace, and His rule is a righteous one—the first completely righteous rule in history. Yet it is not a soft rule. He rules with an iron club—and evildoers must swiftly toe the line. And this is where the weakness lies, not in the rule itself, and certainly not in Christ, but in the inherent soulish nature of the old humanity, which, though technically destroyed at the cross, still remains with mankind until they come to accept the deliverance provided by the cross and become a new creation in Christ. This they will not do during the millennial era, for as soon as the rule is lifted and Satan is released for a time, he is able to enlist vast numbers of earth's inhabitants in a final rebellion.

Let us bear in mind that all the eons, except the final one, end in failure and disaster, and each in increasing measure. The first brought on the disruption, the second the deluge. The present wicked eon closes in the awful judgments of the apocalypse. But the worst failure of all will be the close of the Millennium.

We must look beyond the Millennium, beyond the great white throne, beyond the new heavens and earth—beyond to the consummation, for perfection and finality, when God is All in all.

Chapter XVII

THE GREAT WHITE THRONE JUDGMENT

And I perceived a great white throne, and Him Who is sitting upon it, from Whose face earth and heaven fled, and no place was found for them.
And I perceived the dead, great and small, standing before the throne. And scrolls were opened, and another scroll was opened, which relates to life. And the dead were judged by that which is written in the scrolls, in accord with their acts.
And the sea gives up the dead in it, and death and the unseen give up the dead in them. And they were condemned, each in accord with their acts. And death and the unseen were cast into the lake of fire. This is the second death—the lake of fire. And if anyone was not found written in the scroll of life, he was cast into the lake of fire (Revelation 20:11-15).

The Scriptures are clear and explicit in revealing the time of this judgment in relation to other events in God's eonian administrations. Immediately after the close of the thousand years' reign and the destruction of the rebellious host of the nations under Satan, the great white throne and He Who is sitting upon it appears, from Whose face earth and heaven flee, and no place is found for them (Revelation 20:11). The great white throne judgment takes place while the former heaven and former earth pass away, and a new heaven and a new earth are created for the fifth and final eon (Revelation 21:1). With the earth and heaven gone, the universal greatness of the throne will so unquestionably manifest God's power and glory to all who stand there, that every iota of doubt and unbelief will be completely banished forever.

The great white throne judgment has no place for those who are members of the ecclesia, which is the body of Christ, for they have all been made alive and have been enjoying eonian life and immortality for more than a millennium. Neither is it for the saints of Israel, and others before, who happened upon the resurrection of life at the very beginning of the millennial reign. It is for all those who remain dead.

There can be no judging in death because, as we have noted, it is an unconscious state akin to sleep. Therefore, the dead are roused for judgment. The Scriptures make it clear that they are not vivified (made alive or "quickened"). For vivify always has a special reference to the return of the spirit from death with the giving life beyond the reach of death by conferring incorruption or immortality. During our Lord's ministry and the apostles' ministry, the widow of Nain's son, Lazarus, and others, were resurrected, but not vivified, and so they died again. So also, before the great white throne, all of humanity who are still in the death state are resurrected and roused to be judged and condemned according to their acts, and then die again, entering into the second death.

The Basis of Judgment

The great white throne judgment concerns mankind in general, the vast majority of whom are outside of any written revelation. God will be paying each one in accord with the personal and social deeds of wickedness among each other, as well as their irreverent offenses toward Him. The judgment will be in keeping with the knowledge of God which they possess during the time and circumstances under which they have lived, whether they followed out the instinct of their conscience for good acts or gave themselves over to the corrupt and lustful practices of the world.

In Romans we have the basis of this judgment marked out so clearly that no one need go astray if we do not read into it demands of which the just Judge does not speak. There it is written:

Yet, in accord with your hardness and unrepentant heart you are hoarding for yourself indignation in the day of indignation and revelation of the just judgment of God, Who will be paying each one in accord with his acts (Romans 2:5, 6).

Let us note that "acts" form the basis of this judgment; grace has no part in it. It is a judgment on merits, and the immediate results are not favorable to those being judged. It is a fundamental truth that "the just by faith shall be living" (Habakkuk 2:4; Romans 1:17; Galatians 3:11; Hebrews 10:38), but these being judged here have neither the righteousness nor the faith to qualify them for life. Hence, at the completion of the judging and punishment, they go into the second death, which is neither endless annihilation nor eternal torment, but a figurative means of purification to enable them to be vivified at the conclusion of the eons. This second death is not endless. After it has served its purpose, death will be abolished through the vivification (or rousing and making alive) of all (I Corinthians 15:22-28, II Tim. 1:10).

Amidst the great slough of corrupt humanity, given over to a disqualified mind, doing that which is not befitting, we have the expressed declarations of Scripture that there were some inspired by better motives who did not participate in the great catalogue of sin and evil, who will receive recognition for their good acts in this judgment. Let us not forget the account of the Ninevites, repenting at the proclamation of Jonah in contrast with the "wicked generation" in our Lord's day, who gave no heed to His proclamation. Christ said of them:

Ninevite men will be standing up in judgment with this generation and they will be condemning it, seeing that they repent at the proclamation of Jonah, and lo! more than Jonah is here! (Luke 11:32).

Then, again, there is the account of the queen of the south, who fitted out a train of camels and traveled possibly a thousand miles to learn the wisdom of Solomon, and our Lord said of her:

The queen of the south will be roused in the judgment with the men of this generation, and will be condemning them, seeing that she came out from the ends of the earth to hear the wisdom of Solomon, and lo! more than Solomon is here! (Luke 11:31).

These Scriptures unmistakably speak of recognition being accorded in the day of judgment to those, who out of the instinct of their hearts, have displayed the action of the law in their good acts. Of these Paul says:

For whenever they of the nations that have no law, by nature may be doing that which the law demands, these, having no law, are a law to themselves, who are displaying the action of the law written in their hearts, their conscience testifying together and their reckonings between one another, accusing or defending them, in the day when God will be judging the hidden things of humanity, according to my evangel, through Jesus Christ (Romans 2:14-16).

Result of the Judgment

The result will be judgment and condemnation in accord with their acts. A severe wage is held forth to all who have wantonly participated in the acts of evil and injustice, as it is written:

Yet to those of faction, and stubborn, indeed, as to the truth, yet persuaded to injustice, indignation and fury, affliction and distress, on every human soul which is effecting evil (Romans 2:8, 9).
. . . And they were condemned each in accord with their acts (Revelation 20:13).

It is before the great white throne itself that Christ Jesus corrects and punishes those who have erred regarding Him, His law, and His promises, for there can be no punishment in the insensate condition of death. The intensity of punishment and its duration are just, according to the standards of the Creator God Who is Love. And it will be well to hold in mind that this day of judgment is not to be thought of as a day of twenty-four hours, but will involve a period of time sufficient for God to justly adjudicate all wrongs. Once this is completed, the punishment ceases and the condemned enter the second death.

Thus, here before the great white throne, all the irreverence and injustice receives just adjudication and all wrongs are made right. After justice is fully meted out to each one, being outside of the realm of faith, the second death takes jurisdiction over them (Revelation 2:11; 20:6).

The Second Death and the Lake of Fire

The lake of fire is obviously a symbolic expression, for death and hades (the realm of the imperceptible) are both cast into it. The phrase occurs five times, all in the Book of Revelation. For the Wild Beast, False Prophet and Satan it represents eonian torment because they are cast into it "living," that is, conscious and able to experience suffering (Revelation 19:20, 20:10). They are the only ones said to be tormented for the eons of the eons in the lake of fire. The Beast and the False Prophet are superhuman, the minions of Satan—for he gives them all their power and authority. The Wild Beast dies and is recalled to life (Revelation 13:3). The False Prophet is endowed with power to give spirit to the image of the Wild Beast (Revelation 13:11-15). This is evidence that they possess vitality unknown to other mortals, and this is secured by lawlessly yielding themselves to Satan. This superhuman, miraculous vitality, by which they are enabled to command the wondering worship of mankind, becomes the cause of the severest and longest punishment in the Scriptures. They are arrested and cast into the fiery lake alive, and exist in its torment for the eons of the eons; that is, until the consummation, when death is abolished and the reconciliation of all is effected.

For irreverent mankind—those not found written in the book of life—the lake of fire is the second death (Revelation 20:14, 15, 21:8); and, since death is a return to a state of complete dissolution and unconsciousness, they have no awareness of time and do not suffer at all in that figurative place. After the great white throne, the next thing those who have been judged and set right are aware of is the consummation when God becomes All in all.

Fire—A Healing Symbol

The common view of fire as only or chiefly a penal agent is very shallow. Fire, in Scripture, is the element of life (Isaiah 4:5), of purification (Matthew 3:11), of atonement (Leviticus 16:27), of transformation (II Peter 3:7-10).

If we take either the teaching of Scripture or of nature, we see that the dominant conception of fire is of a beneficent agent. Nature tells us that fire is a necessary condition of life; its mission is to sustain life; and to purify, even when it dissolves. Extinguish the stores of fire in the universe, and you extinguish all being; universal death and darkness reigns. The connection between fire and life show in the facts of nutrition. For we actually burn in order to live; our food is the fuel; our bodies are furnaces; our nutrition is a process of combustion; we are, in fact, aflame to the very tips of our fingers. And so it is that around the fireside that life and work gather.

And what nature teaches, Scripture positively reinforces. It is significant to find the Great Source of all life constantly associated with fire in the Word. Fire is the sign, not of God's wrath, but of His Being. When God comes to Ezekiel, there is "fire unfolding itself" (1:4, 27), and the "appearance of fire" (8:2). The eyes of Christ are as a "flame of fire" (Revelation 1:14). And the "seven torches of fire burning before the throne" are "the seven spirits of God" (Revelation 4:5). A fiery stream is said "to go before God," His throne is fiery flame, its wheels are burning fire, and His eyes are lamps of fire (Daniel 7:6-10). He is a wall of fire (Zechariah 2:5). At His touch the mountains smoke (Psalms 104:32). God's ministers are a flame of fire (Psalms 104:5, Hebrews 1:7).

It is not meant to deny that the divine fire chastises and destroys. It is meant that purification, not ruin, is the final outcome of that fire from above, which consumes—call it, if you wish, a paradox—in order that it may save. For if God be Love and Light, then by what except by Love and Light can His fires be kindled?

Let us note, also, how often fire is the sign of a favorable answer from God. When God appears to Moses at the Bush, it is in fire. God answers Gideon by fire, and David by fire (I Chronicles 21:26). Again, when He answers Elijah on Carmel, it is by fire, and in fire that God transports Elijah. So God sends to Elisha chariots and horses of fire. So when the Psalmist calls, God answers by fire (Psalms 18:6-8). And by the pillar of fire, God guides the Israelites through the wilderness, and in fire God gave His law. And in fire the great gift of Pentecost descends.

Also in the Greek Scriptures we find that fire, like judgment, so far from being the sinner's portion only, is the portion of all. Like God's judgment again, it is not future merely, but present; it is "already kindled," i.e., always kindled: its object is not torment, but cleansing. The proof comes from the lips of our Lord Himself. "I am come to send fire on the earth," words that in fact convey all I am seeking to teach, for it is certain that He came as Saviour of the "whole world" (I John 2:2). Thus, coming to save, Christ comes with fire already kindled. He comes to baptize with the Holy Spirit, and with fire. Therefore, it is that Christ teaches in a solemn passage (usually misunderstood Mark 9:43) that every one shall be salted with fire. And so the "fire is to try every man's work." He whose work fails is saved (mark the word saved), not damned "so as by fire," for God's fire, by consuming what is evil, saves and refines.

And so echoing Deuteronomy 4:24-31, we are told that "Our God is a consuming fire"—a consuming fire by which the whole material substance of sin is destroyed. When, then, we read in Psalms 18:12-13 that "coals of fire" go before God, we think of the deeds of love which are coals of fire to our enemies (Romans 12:20). Thus we who teach hope for all men, do not shrink from but accept, in their fullest meaning, these mysterious fires of Gehenna, of which Christ speaks (kindled for purification), as in a special sense the sinner's doom in the coming eon. But taught by the clearest statements of Scripture (confirmed as they are by many analogies of nature), we see in these fires not a denial of, but a mode of fulfilling, the promise, "Behold, I make all things new."

The Basic Question

The question is not whether those who die in unbelief are lost. "He who is believing in the Son has life eonian, yet he who is stubborn as to the Son shall not be seeing life, but the indignation of God is remaining on Him" (John 3:36). The question is not whether the unbeliever is lost, or whether he is subject to divine wrath, or even to the second death as well. The question is just one thing: Is the second death the unbeliever's final end?

We need not ask whether there is a second death, but whether there is life subsequent to the second death—for those who were cast into the lake of fire. The true answer to this question can only be found in the will and counsel of God, according to the design of the cross. In the Book of Revelation, the apostle John simply does not address this question; instead it is left for the apostle Paul to settle, through his own ministry, which completes the word of God, and thus all prophecy (Col. 1:25).

According to Paul, Christ's saving work is a matter of gratuitous grace (Romans 5:15), not of human qualification. Accordingly, then, since God will abolish death at the end of the eons, and the only death operative at that time is the second death, it follows that the second death will be abolished, so that God, the One who makes light and darkness, good and evil, will be All in all of his creatures (I Corinthians 15:28).

Denominational Misunderstandings

Because of the many Bible mistranslations and false teachings of Christendom, we must make a revolutionary revision of our entire

123

outlook in regard to the future fate of the unbeliever. We need a God's-eye view instead of man's. The great white throne judging is not a futile attempt to deal out punishment to those who have already suffered and who will be tormented endlessly, without any regard to God's purpose in creation or the effect on His great name. It is His means of manifesting to men their utter failure to give Him His due. It will convince them that His sentence, condemning every son of Adam (Romans 5:18), is just and true. And it will also reveal His righteousness in Christ, Who will be their Judge, by means of which all can and will be justified, and thus the solid ground laid down for their reconciliation at the consummation, the end of the eons.

The substitution of eternal torture for universal reconciliation has utterly distorted every aspect of the great white throne judging. This diabolical doctrine changes the motive of judgment from love to hate. Instead of a marvelous display of God's ability to help His creatures, it is debased to a vicious exhibition of His power to harm. Tremendous might is exercised in order to raise the dead, with no other reason than to associate their dire doom with Christ and His God. Few of them had ever seen Him. Most of them had never heard of Him. Now they are to exist forever in unutterable, unending torture, as a result of their meeting with the Saviour of the whole world! What motive can there be for connecting a Saviour with such dire punishment? Is he there to mock them, to intensify their despair, to multiply their misery? If the uniform penalty of all who stand before the great white throne is eternal torment, then Satan, not Christ, should preside. The adversary, not the Saviour, should sit as judge.

Eternal torment makes the judging at the great white throne futile and foolish. Universal reconciliation makes it fruitful and wise. What profit is it to God to torment His creatures endlessly, when, if He is the Deity of limitless power and infinite wisdom, He could save them and get from them the fruit of His labors, and enjoy the worship and adoration for which He created them? What are we to think of a God Who would create billions of creatures to curse Him endlessly? No man would exert such power in order to turn his own handiwork against himself, unless he were demented. Why charge God with this insanity?

White, Not Black

The color of the judgment throne relates to the outcome of the judging. Eternal torment demands that it be black. Reconciliation calls for white. The lives of most men are drab with toil and trouble, disease and death. If this is to be followed by an eternity of agony, surely no hue but the dankest ebony could possibly accord with the tragedies to be enacted there. Black alone could properly depict the horrible fate to which everyone who stands before it is hopelessly damned. But white is the color of light and righteousness and holiness. Our Lord's garments "became white as the light" on the mount of transformation (Matthew 17:2). The messengers, commonly called "angels," are clothed in white (Matthew 28:3, John 20:12, Acts 1:10). Worthy saints are robed in white (Revelation 3:4, 5, 7:9, 13, 19:14). They whiten their garments in the blood of the Lambkin (Revelation 7:14).

Black is the symbol of darkness and death. The present is a time of blackness and darkness. Men love darkness because their deeds are evil (John 3:19). Even we were once darkness (Ephesians 5:5). This era is actually called "darkness," because that is its chief characteristic (Ephesians 6:12).

All Unbelievers Set Right

There is no great white throne today. There is no divine standard of righteousness. As in a blackout, men grope their way about. They commit their shameful deeds in secret, unseen by their fellows. If there were such a white tribunal on earth, it would put an end to all this. No one would be able to hide. All would be open. Even our departure from God, our failure to give Him His right place in our lives, would be painfully exposed. On the other hand, is not this just what we sigh for when appalled by the prevailing wickedness? We are right, there should be light thrown into this darkness. Everything should be exposed and set right. That is what reformers aim to do. It will be done, but not now. That is the function of the great white throne.

But it will not be a mere reformation in which wickedness is punished and good rewarded. All will be condemned because they are not merely compared with their fellows, but with the glory of God, where all fall short. Not only will all be found guilty, but all will be set right—

for this is the true meaning of judgment—not only with their human associates, but with God, to whom they owe infinitely more than to their neighbors.

Every human being, and, indeed, every living thing, is an exquisite and costly creation of God, infinitely more valuable than the highest achievements of human skill. Man cannot impart life or growth or sensation to any of his creations. All that he can do is to destroy these. What man would not do his utmost to save the work of a lifetime from destruction? And will not God do all that He can to reclaim the lost? Indeed, has He not already done all that is needed to protect His holiness in the sacrifice of Christ? The value of that offering is great enough to include all mankind, and embrace all creation. Now that the price has been paid, the ransom for all laid down, what can God do except to honor the work of Christ and apply the preciousness of His blood to those for whom it was shed? A judgment is just what is needed to accomplish this, where all who have not been won by faith will be reached by sight. There all the wrongs of His creatures will be righted, and they will see how inutterably they have wronged Him. Thus they will be brought to realize that God alone is their All. What sane person would not welcome being "set right," and prepared for endless life of perfection by our Loving Creator? God is Light, and it is His Light which emanates from the great white throne. Once we realize what judging means in the Word of God, that it is a corrective measure of the Supreme God of Love and Light, the great white throne becomes a pledge of universal reconciliation, not of eternal damnation.

The great white throne judgment is not due until all men who will die have done so. Otherwise there would need to be a repetition of it. This is not necessary, for as we shall see, with the creation of the new heaven and new earth at the beginning of the eon of the eons, men will no longer die. There will be no more dying. But the second death is not yet abolished.

Chapter XVIII

THE EON OF THE EONS

Now the day of the Lord will be arriving as a thief, in which the heavens shall be passing by with a booming noise, yet the elements shall be dissolved by combustion, and the earth and the works in it shall be found. At these all, then, dissolving, to what manner of men must you belong in holy behaviour and devoutness, hoping for and hurrying the presence of God's day, because of which the heavens, being on fire, will be dissolved, and the elements decompose by combustion! Yet we, according to His promises, are hoping for new heavens and a new earth, in which righteousness is dwelling (II Peter 3:10-13).

And I perceived a new heaven and a new earth, for the former heaven and the former earth pass away, and the sea is no more.
And I perceived the holy city, new Jerusalem, descending out of heaven from God, made ready as a bride adorned for her husband. And I hear a loud voice out of the throne saying, "Lo! the tabernacle of God is with mankind, and he will be tabernacling with them, and they will be His peoples, and God Himself will be with them. And he will be brushing away every tear from their eyes. And death will be no more, nor mourning, nor clamor, nor misery; they will be no more, for the former things passed away."
And He Who is sitting on the throne said, "Lo! New am I making all!" And He is saying, "Write, for these sayings are faithful and true" (Revelation 21:1-5).

At the time of the great white throne judgment, the Supreme Subjector dissolves the world by fire creating new heavens and a new earth, bringing on the presence of "God's day," the most glorious and wonderful of the eonian times. During the Millennium, righteousness *rules* the earth. During the new creation, righteousness *dwells* upon the earth (II Peter 3:13, Revelation 21:3).

Now comes the great fulfillment of the promise to Abraham and Israel from God. "By faith [Abraham] sojourns in the land of promise as in an alien land, dwelling in tabernacles with Isaac and Jacob, the joint enjoyers of the allotment of the same promise. For he waited for the city having foundations, whose Artificer and Architect is God" (Hebrews 11:9-10).

The Supreme Artificer and Architect brings New Jerusalem out of heaven. Its very character is heavenly, and it comes to earth. It is four square, and on side measures 12,000 stadia (Revelation 21:16-17). Since 1 stadium equals 606.75 feet, that makes the holy city approximately 1,500 miles wide, 1,500 miles long, and 1,500 miles high. It takes up an area about half the size of the continental United States. On the portals of the New Jerusalem are inscribed the names of the twelve tribes of the sons of Israel. And . . .

The foundations of the wall of the city are adorned with every precious stone, the first foundation with jasper, the second lapis lazuli, the third chalcedony, the fourth emerald, the fifth sardonyx, the sixth carnelian, the seventh topaz, the eighth beryl, the ninth peridot, the tenth chrysoprase, the eleventh amethyst, the twelfth garnet. And the twelve portals are twelve pearls. Each one of the portals was respectively of one pearl. And the square of the city is gold, clear as translucent glass.

And a temple I did not perceive in it, for the Lord God Almighty is its temple, and the Lambkin. And the city has no need of the sun nor of the moon, that they should be appearing in it, for the glory of God illuminates it, and its lamp is the Lambkin (Revelation 21:19-23).

This last eon is the longest and the most excellent. It is life-filled, light-flooded, and love-lavished. Until we grasp some of its magnificent grandeur, as compared with the previous eons, we will fail to feel the force of its name, and think of it merely as later and better, not the very greatest and grandest and most glorious of the eonian times. As our view of the eons as a whole depends partly on our apprehension of its overwhelming proportions, we will try to discover, if we can, something about its magnitude, the vast period of time which it takes up, the innumerable host of inhabitants, and the superlative condition of humanity when death will be absent and God present in the earth.

The Length of the Last Eon

We know that the Millennium, or day of Yahweh, will somewhat exceed a thousand years, but we have no such clear statement concerning the last eon. At best then, we can only guess based on scriptural evidence. It makes sense that the fifth and final eon would be longer than the second, third, and fourth combined. It agrees with our spiritual instincts, for God is swift in His judgments, but prolongs the dispensation of His favors. As we can already see, the last eon will be one of unexampled earthly blessedness. God's heart will be able to rest in it. Its length may well exceed all that went before, from the time of Adam.

In the King James Version, we read of the glory of the church "throughout all ages, world without end. Amen" (Ephesians 3:21). Behind this misleading translation are words that flood the last eon with light. The entire verse ought to read, "to Him be glory in the ecclesia and in Christ Jesus for all the generations of the eon of the eons! Amen!" So seldom is the eon of the eons specially singled out like this that this passage must be considered one of the prime sources of information concerning it. The principal point is very striking. In the final eon, the eon of the eons, there will be *generations*. Mankind will continue to multiply. Time will be marked by recurring births. New members of the human race will be continually added to it.

How many generations will there be? Some idea of the number will enable us to form a rough estimate of the eon's length. The psalmist speaks of a thousand generations from Adam to the end of the eons (Psalms 105:8). The length of a single generation could hardly average under twenty years. This would give the total time of humanity's existence from Adam (the beginning of the second eon) to the consummation as twenty thousand years. Since Adam, we have probably made about six thousand years of history. The next eon will account for more than a thousand years. This leaves about thirteen thousand years for the final eon.

If we conservatively allot only half of the thousand generations of humanity to the last eon, we see that the proportionate population of the new earth will be beyond all estimate. Even if it should begin with a single pair, as Adam and Eve started the chain in the previous eons, it would baffle calculation, for there will be no death, not even disease or strife to diminish the number of earth's denizens. The point is this: by far the greater part of mankind in the eons is found in the last of the series, and these humans know little of the distress that we experience, for there will be no doom and no death. While it is true that those who stand before the great white throne will make up an enormous assemblage, including all the unsaved dead from Adam down, it is most likely that the population of the earth at the end of the eon of the eons will dwarf their number.

The Third Heaven Above Paradise

In II Corinthians 12:2, Paul reveals that he has had what we would today refer to as an out-of-body experience, having been "snatched away to the third heaven." This most probably happened fourteen years before he penned this epistle, at Lystra, where he was stoned and left for dead. As A. E. Knoch writes in the *Concordant Commentary*:

Paul entered the third heaven and there saw (what he afterward revealed in his perfection epistles—Ephesians, Philippians and Colossians) the universal supremacy of Christ and the supernal dignity conferred on the ecclesia which is Christ's body. He also enters the new earth and its park, which John describes [in Revelation 21]. All of this he had seen, but he was not allowed to disclose it until the time was ripe. This came when Israel's apostasy was full blown, as recorded at the close of the book of Acts. Till then he does not even claim to be the man who had seen and heard such transcendent revelations.

While undoubtedly we will visit the new earth in our immortal bodies of light and marvel at the great splendor and peace of this paradise, the abode and viewpoint of the ecclesia which is Christ's body will remain celestial during this most magnificent of the eons. But let's get back to earth.

Dwellers on the New Earth

Where do the dwellers on the new earth come from? The fact that they are called mankind (Revelation 21:3) shows that they are the same individuals as were on the former earth. Since the names of the twelve tribes of the sons of Israel are inscribed on the portals of the new Jerusalem, we know all the saints in Israel will be there.

The Scriptures do not relate the manner in which these are carried over from the former to the new earth. There is no new vivification, but those who receive eonian life at the beginning of the Millennium will doubtless be there, including all the saints of past time outside the celestial allotment. Besides these vivified saints, we read of only two classes, the nations (Revelation 21:24) and the new Jerusalem, in which the holy nation will have its habitation. Among these we may find the generations of which the psalmist and our own Paul prophesied.

Mortality and the Tree of Life

We must remember, however, that mankind still will be linked with Adam, death will still be transmitted, and those born will be mortals, whose life will be a process of dying. How then can there be no more death? This is managed by a special provision, which is one of the features of this eon of the eons. In the garden of Eden was the tree of life (Genesis 3:22). Had Adam had access to it he could have prolonged his life indefinitely. Hence he was driven out, and cherubim were set to guard the way to the tree of life. It is evident from this that a tree of life can counteract the effects of mortality. It imparts life, which is the opposite of the death operating in us. God did not wish Adam to live. In the last eon, He does wish the sons of mankind to live. So He provides a tree of life in the very center of the paradise to come, and it will be the portion of all the conquerors in Ephesus (Revelation 2:7), as well as all Israel who attain that era.

In the new earth there will be far more. There will be the river of water of life, resplendent as crystal, issuing out of the throne of God and the Lambkin. Not only will its vitalizing flood check the deadly virus of Adamic death, but there will be the tree of life, in vast numbers apparently, on either side of it, and Israel will be partakers of its monthly fruit, while the nations will be cured by its leaves. It would seem that the trees draw this life-giving fluid from the river of life, whose crystal tide flows from the throne of God and the Lambkin. How significant! God is the source of all life, but the life eonian comes alone by the channel of the sacrificial Lambkin. This life is not a reward from God for works, but a gracious gift that comes to mankind through the death of His Son.

No More Doom

As we have seen, God is the great *Placer*. The Greek element *-the-* denotes PLACE, and *Theos,* the name of God, from which we get *The*ology, and many like words, denotes the One Who places. This may have been a translation, originally, of the Hebrew *Eloah*, from the root *El*, DISPOSE or SUBJECT, for it denotes practically the same, the Disposer or Subjector. Even unbelievers have the proverb, "Man proposes: God disposes," which gives an excellent idea of the basic nature of Deity.

In this same family, PLACE, there is a very interesting word that deals with God's placing or disposing. This is *kata-the-ma*, DOWN-PLACE-*effect*, doom. The element kata, DOWN, sometimes has the idea of adverseness, as DOWN JUST, convict; DOWN ABLE, tyrannize; DOWN JUDGE, condemn; DOWN TALK, speak against; DOWN EXECRATE, curse. So in the word doom, it seems to have almost the literal sense of *place* in a *down*ward position. The potter has a right to make a vessel for dishonor. The clay has no right to object. If God wishes to display His indignation and make His power known, He has the right to make appropriate vessels of indignation suited to destruction (Romans 9:22, 23). This He does during the eons that precede the great white throne judgment. In the last eon, however, God has already made known His indignation against sin. His power has been fully displayed. As the great Potter, He finds no more call for vessels of indignation. All are vessels of mercy adapted to display His glory. There is no more DOWN-PLACE-effect: there is no more doom (Revelation 22:3).

The fact that God no more dooms His creatures to display His inevitable yet dreadful indignation, nor, as He did with Pharaoh, places them in positions of power that He may display His own, gives the eon of the eons a character radically diverse from the three before it, even the much lauded Millennium. It is a mistake to suppose that God's present activities are normal, or that they will be eternal. In the second, third, and fourth eons, He dooms some of His creatures, to undergo evils, in order to display His attributes. At the great white throne judgment, any apparent wrong is fully righted, so that none of His creatures will ever hold it against Him. This activity of His does not enter the last eon.

When we consider the untold hosts of His creatures in the concluding eon on the earth, as well as the countless company in other confines of the universe, all of whom will be spectators of the tragedy of the eons, especially the middle three, and compare their number with the small fraction who are upon the center of the stage during these eons, even though their sum seems large to us, they dwindle down to insignificance, and we find ourselves viewing the evil of the eons much as Paul looked upon our personal experience. Even when we endure a long life of suffering, by comparison, we may speak of it as a "momentary, light affliction" which ultimately produces for us a "transcendently transcendent eonian burden of glory" (II Corinthians 4:17). This expression also carries with it the implication that the last eon is of great length and glory, for the preceding one is too short and ends with much evil on the earth, not warranting these superlative expressions.

No More Night

We read that night will be no more (Revelation 22:5). That this is literal is evident from the fact that lamps will not be needed, nor even sunlight. Just how the Lord will illuminate the new earth is not explained. Yet in the past, the appearance of heavenly visitants, endowed with superabundant vitality, when allowed to shine forth, has been bright with light. Our Lord hid His glory, except when He was seen on the mount of transformation, or when Saul saw Him on the way to Damascus. Then the light was blinding in its intensity. The glory of God shone about the messenger who announced the birth of the Saviour to the shepherds (Luke 2:9). Even today, many fishes carry with them a means of illumination in the dark depths of the sea. It is therefore quite possible that the bold figure of the apostle Paul, "you are light in the Lord" (Ephesians 5:8) will not only become fact in our case, among the celestials, but may also be true of the dwellers on the earth in the eons of the eons.

The illumination seems to apply particularly to His servants in Israel, who, as the passage provides, will reign for the eons of the eons. The nations will walk by the light of the holy Jerusalem (Revelation 21:24). Undoubtedly this luminous exterior will correspond with an enlightened heart and mind. All will know God then, especially His servants, for, it is significantly added, they will offer Him the service which is His due (Revelation 22:3). He is their light and their illumination in a sense far deeper than the visible brilliance of their frames, for this is the great prerequisite to becoming their All.

Life is needed before men can have light, and light goes before love. So the Supreme Subjector and Placer will reveal Himself in the eon of the eons, not by the dark contrasts of sin and Satan, but by the increasing life, the brightening light, the positive lavishing of His love. The superabundant life and the unlimited light of this final eon approach the glories of the consummation with its supreme revelation of God's boundless love.

Chapter XIX

THE CONSUMMATION—THE END OF THE EONS

Wherefore, also, God highly exalts Him, and graces Him with the name that is above every name, that in the name of Jesus every knee should be bowing, celestial and terrestrial and subterranean, and every tongue should be acclaiming that Jesus Christ is Lord, for the glory of God, the Father (Philippians 2: 9-11).

For even as, in Adam, all are dying, thus also, in Christ, shall all be vivified. Yet each in his own class: the Firstfruit, Christ; there upon those who are Christ's in His presence; thereafter the consummation, whenever He may be giving up the kingdom to His God and Father, whenever He should be nullifying all sovereignty and all authority and power. For he must be reigning until He should be placing all His enemies under His feet. The last enemy being abolished: death. For He subjects all under His feet. Now whenever He may be saying that all is subject, it is evident that it is outside of Him Who subjects all to Him. Now, whenever all may be subjected to Him, the Son Himself also shall be subjected to Him Who subjects all to Him, that God may be All in all (I Corinthians 15: 22-28).

Many of us have attended high school or college reunions. They can be a lot of fun, but often the people we had hoped to see most are not there. Not so at the Great Reunion of humanity at the end of the eons. Everyone will be there. All unbelievers who became believers at the great white throne will join us there. The Supreme Spirit brings them out of their unconsciousness in the second death. During the eon of the eons, death became "no more." Now, it is *abolished*. Since the second death is the only death remaining, all in it are brought out of it into immortal life. The True God completes His work of reconciling a universe that He had intentionally set at enmity to Himself, so that His very essence might be known and experienced by all.

Before the eons, sin and evil were unknown. At the end of the eons, sin and evil are also absent but well-known. When God becomes All in all His creations, all are filled with Spirit, Light, and Love. The Scriptures do not speak of what happens then. We are free to meditate upon this coming unspeakable joy. We can imagine all the wonderful things in store for us. But even then, our minds and spirits will not grasp the exceeding glories to come, for the True God "is able to do superexcessively above all that we are requesting or apprehending, according to the power that is operating in us" (Ephesians 3:20).

There is no longer a need for a Saviour. There is no need for a King after God becomes "All in all." At the consummation, all sovereignty, authority, and power are nullified. Our last scene of all is sometimes termed "The Great Abdication." For when all are gathered together in Christ—when all in the universe are subjected to Him—when every creature acknowledges His sovereignty and acclaims Him as Lord—when all hail the power of Jesus' name and even angels prostrate fall—then, what happens? Christ steps down, and hands over all to God, His Father, that God may be All in all.

Can you imagine any lesser potentate being willing to hand over so much? But surely the grandeur of God's purpose lies essentially in the supreme confidence which the Father has in the Son of His love. God can invest all in Christ in the full knowledge that all will be handed back to Him. God can exalt Christ to the very highest pinnacle in the universe in the absolute certainty that His Son will never seek to usurp the Father's position. God the Father "wills that all mankind be saved and come into a realization of the truth," and Christ descended from heaven and went to the cross to accomplish His Father's will (John 6:39).

There is no longer a need for a Mediator of God and mankind. No longer is the Supreme Spirit outside His creations, but fully in them. All in all! None of God's creatures remains outside the scope of His indwelling; nothing outside of God Himself dwells in any of His creatures! This is the climax of all prophecy. It explains its purpose and solves its puzzles. Our existence makes sense. Thus God's purpose, once intensely contracted and concentrated, so that it was all brought to focus in one Man suspended from a pole as a malefactor, now expands again to take in the utmost limits of creation. Truly God's thoughts and ways are not ours, but infinitely more lofty; and how grand His purpose is, in its conception, in its outworking, and in its glorious fulfillment! In every stage it serves to glorify the One Whose purpose is being accomplished.

We have often read of the abdication of earthly monarchs—some because of ill health and bodily weakness, some because of misrule, and others through lack of power to hold the obedience and loyalty of their subjects. But at the consummation of God's eonian purpose we read of a glorious abdication the like of which has never been entertained by any of earth's monarchs. The reign of Christ comes to an end because He has brought all to His Father. The active exhibition of such glories as might (I Peter 4:11, 5:11; Revelation 1:6, 5:13) and power (Revelation 7:12) become obsolete because they have been perfectly administered. The love He demonstrates at Cavalry to humanity and to all celestial beings, ultimately brings the universe to a heavenly state of loving subjection. Think of a reign so beneficent that all is brought to such a state of perfection that the need of restraints of any kind vanishes!

Truly, "The LORD is good to all: and His tender mercies are over all His works" (Psalms 145:9). Let us rejoice in the truth that the fate of individual humans and the destiny of humanity as a whole is not settled by man's religions or by death, but by the Supreme Spirit of Light and Love through Christ Jesus our Lord.

Chapter XX

A SCRIPTURAL SUMMARY

The best way to review the teaching of this book is to return directly to the source upon which it is based—the Sacred Scriptures:

... [T]here is one God [Who] is Spirit (John 4:24), Light (I John 1:5), [and] Love (I John 4:8), and one Mediator of God and mankind, a Man, Christ Jesus (I Timothy 2:5-6), Who is the Image of the invisible God, Firstborn of every creature, for in Him is all created, that in the heavens and that on the earth, the visible and the invisible, whether thrones, or lordships, or sovereignties, or authorities, all is created through Him and for Him, and He is before all, and all has its cohesion in Him (Colossians 1:15-17).

Christ died for our sins according to the scriptures, and ... He was entombed, and ... He has been roused the third day according to the scriptures (I Corinthians 15:3-4).

All scripture is inspired by God, and is beneficial for teaching (II Timothy 3:16). Every word of God is pure (Proverbs 30:5). [We] beware that no one shall be despoiling [us] through philosophy and empty seduction, in accord with human tradition, in accord with the elements of the world, and not in accord with Christ, for in Him the entire complement of the Deity is dwelling bodily (Colossians 2:8, 9).

[We] endeavor to present [ourselves] to God qualified, unashamed worker[s], correctly cutting the word of truth (II Timothy 2:15), [having] a pattern of sound words, which [we] hear from [Paul], in faith and love in Christ Jesus (II Timothy 1:13), [understanding that Paul has] been entrusted with the evangel of the Uncircumcision [the nations], according as Peter of the Circumcision [Israel] (Galations 2:7).

To [Paul], less than the least of all saints, was granted this grace: to bring the evangel of the untraceable riches of Christ to the nations, and to enlighten all as to what is the administration of the secret, which has been concealed from the eons in God, Who creates all, that now may be made known to the sovereignties and the authorities among the celestials, through the ecclesia, the multifarious wisdom of God, in accord with the purpose of the eons, which He makes in Christ Jesus, our Lord; in Whom we have boldness and access with confidence, through His faith (Ephesians 3:8-12).

It is not ours to wrestle with blood and flesh, but with the sovereignties, with the authorities, with the world-mights of this darkness, with the spiritual forces of wickedness among the celestials (Ephesians 6:12).

We rely on the living God, Who is the Saviour of all mankind, especially of believers (I Timothy 4:10). For even as, in Adam, all are dying, thus also, in Christ, shall all be vivified. Yet each in his own class: the Firstfruit, Christ; thereupon those who are Christ's in His presence; thereafter the consummation ... Now, whenever all may be subject to Him, then the Son Himself also shall be subjected to Him Who subjects all to Him, that God may be All in all (I Corinthians 15: 22-23, 28).

For in grace, through faith, are [we] saved, and this is not out of [us]; it is God's approach present, not of works, lest anyone should be boasting. For His achievement are we, being created in Christ Jesus for good works, which God makes ready beforehand, that we should be walking in them (Ephesians 2:8-10).

Yet all is of God, Who conciliates us to Himself through Christ, and is giving us the dispensation of the conciliation, how that God was in Christ, conciliating the world to Himself, not reckoning their offenses to them, and placing in us the word of conciliation. For Christ, then, are we ambassadors, as of God entreating through us. We are beseeching for Christ's sake, "Be conciliated to God!" (II Corinthians 5:18-20).

... [I]f anyone is in Christ, there is a new creation ... (II Corinthians 5:17), [f]or our realm is inherent in the heavens, out of which we are awaiting a Saviour also, the Lord, Jesus Christ, Who will transfigure the body of our humiliation, to conform it to the body of His glory, in accord with the operation which enables Him even to subject all to Himself (Philippians 3:20, 21).

[We entreat] then, first of all, that petitions, prayers, pleadings, thanksgiving be made for all mankind, for kings and all those being in a superior station, that we may be leading a mild and quiet life in all devoutness and gravity, for this is ideal and welcome in the sight of our Saviour, God, Who wills that all mankind be saved and come into a realization of the truth (I Timothy 2:1-4).

Now to the King of the eons, the incorruptible, invisible, only, and wise God, be honor and glory for the eons of the eons! Amen! (I Timothy 1:17).

You may wish to compare this scriptural review with the man-made Athanasian Creed on page 33. Does not the Supreme Spirit's Truth radiate Light and "dis-spell" the darkness?

Chapter XXI

AFTERTHOUGHTS AND CREDITS

An Analogy

We can compare the Word of God in its original form to a temple made of perfectly cut white marble blocks. Each block fits in its proper place without the need of mortar. Using these original blocks, we find that there is no room for error because, obviously, God did not build any room for error into His temple of truth—and the end result is a masterpiece of architecture from the Infallible Architect. Everything fits perfectly. Taken together, all the words and concepts which the blocks represent make perfect sense. And within this great temple, it is our privileged delight to "rely on the living God, Who is the Savior of all mankind, especially of believers" (I Timothy 4:10). We can feel confident and secure, resting in God's Spirit, Love, Light and Truth.

The myriad man-made temples of Christendom, by comparison, are spotted with confusion and contradictions. Salvation, instead of pertaining to "all mankind," pertains only to the few, and for the most part, is obtained by jumping through an arbitrary series of hoops depending on the denomination. And this salvation is a very "iffy" matter. What if the Jehovah's Witnesses are right? Or the Mormons? What if the pope really is the Vicar of Christ? What if you need to be baptized by immersion to be saved? Or speak in tongues? Or accept a certain creed? Or attend church services more often? Or confess all of your sins? Or be "born again?"

The reason there is so much variance throughout Christendom is that the diverse Christian sects prefer to build their own flawed temples rather than to abide in God's already established and perfected one. They do indeed use many of the perfect white marble blocks, but some they replace with marred blocks imperfectly cut by their own hands. Some are even a different hue, and some have cracks in them. Some are made of clay. Instead of allowing that the words in the Sacred Scriptures already fit perfectly, they try to fit in all their irregular blocks with the perfectly cut ones. Sometimes they force a true block into the wrong place. They wrench the blocks they deem most important from their proper places and stack them near the entrance, usually with a big sign.

To make a single structure out of all these imperfectly fitting blocks, they need to stir up some mortar—the equivalent of their own philosophies and myths. And so we wind up with 200 (or however many different denominations there are) very different-looking temples. Each has many pure blocks of truth in it, but all of the temples are botched up with blocks of thought that are out of place or do not belong at all. And then the human builders of these various temples begin to believe that the mortar they use to assemble the blocks has more truth and saving power than the original and pure blocks themselves. But still, within each one of these denominational temples, beneath the dogma, the truth is there.

In I Corinthians 11:19, the apostle Paul explains to us that there is a reason for the many different and imperfectly fashioned temples of belief: "For it must be that there are sects also among you, that those also who are qualified may be becoming apparent among you." Sect is the Greek word *hairesis* and it means preference. What is your religious preference? Roman Catholic? Lutheran? Pentecostal? Unitarian? Baptist? As Paul writes in Galations 5:19-21, sects and strife and factions and dissensions are all works of the flesh, not of the spirit. But again, within each one of the Christian sects, the truth is there, hidden beneath our "preferences" and disagreements.

The Concordant Publishing Concern

Mr. A. E. Knoch (1874-1965), the co-founder, with Vladimir M. Gelesnoff (1877-1921), of the Concordant Publishing Concern began to understand these things in the early decades of the twentieth century. It became his lifetime work to give the English reader access to the original manuscripts, eliminate the bias of the translator, and present the True God's temple of truth as it stands in the Sacred Scriptures.

In his early studies of the Sacred Scriptures, he used Greek and Hebrew concordances to get past the mistranslations to the truth. But, in his own words, it was . . .

> **trying, tedious toil. I could not expect others to spend so much time and labor in order to conform their Bible to the inspired original. So I was**

burdened with a tremendous urge to make a concordant version, which would save so much work and give the Lord's dear saints access to God's Word, free from the prejudice which pops up on nearly every page of the Authorized Version, which, as every concordance will show, was made without any method, and was motivated principally by professional theologians who had to please King James.

Thanks to his pioneering, inspired, and dedicated work, all of us now have access to a temple of truth nearly perfectly built—one without cracked or clay blocks, and without any man-made mortar fashioned to hold discordant translations together.

The Concordant Publishing Concern's bi-monthly magazine, *Unsearchable Riches*, has now been published for more than one hundred continuous years. More than twenty years ago, I obtained all the back issues available, some going back to the 1920s. All of the writers for it have possessed a deep knowledge of the Scriptures. My mind and my spirit feasted upon every issue. Much of this book, especially chapters VI through XII, XV and XVIII, contains the writing of Mr. Knoch out of the pages of *Unsearchable Riches*. When I first started taking notes, I thought I would be able to re-express what he wrote in my own words. But I almost always found that I was not able to do so. Other writers for the magazine and for other Concordant publications whose sentences, paragraphs, and sometimes more, appear in this book include, Vladimir M. Gelesnoff, Adlai Loudy, Dean Hough, Cecil J. Blay, Dr. Loyal F. Hurley, William Mealand, John H. Essex, Thomas Allin, Herman Rocke, James Coram, and many more.

It is right that the work of these men should appear here because, after all, they are my teachers. My goal in compiling, editing, organizing and adding to this material has never been to be "original," but rather to be faithful to the original Scriptures and our One Teacher, as these men have been.

Knowledge and Love

This knowledge of the Supreme Spirit's grace and His superlative purpose for humanity is a gift of inestimable value, but it is not enough to take us into Christian maturity. For if I "should be perceiving all secrets and all knowledge, and if I should have all faith, so as to transport mountains, yet have not love, I am nothing" (I Corinthians 13:2). Nothing!

The last thing we want to do is start some new sect or religion. We should rather season, with our knowledge and love, those with which we may come in contact, for they all play a part in the Supreme Spirit's purpose. Let's leave our work and the results of it to Him, since, as He tells us in Isaiah 55:10, 11:

> **For not as My devices are your devices,**
> **And not as your ways are My ways . . .**
> **For as the heavens are loftier than the earth,**
> **So are my ways loftier than your ways,**
> **And My devices than your devices.**
> **For, as descending is the downpour and the snow from the heavens,**
> **Yet there it is not returning, but rather soaks the earth,**
> **And causes it to bear and to sprout,**
> **And gives seed to the sower and bread to the eater,**
> **So shall be My word which shall fare forth from My mouth.**
> **It shall not return to Me empty,**
> **But rather, it does that which I desire,**
> **And prospers in that for which I sent it.**

Made in the USA
Middletown, DE
24 July 2024

57659771R00087